BILL MILLER'S
RIVIERA

TOM AUSTIN & RON KASE

BILL MILLER'S
RIVIERA

AMERICA'S SHOWPLACE
IN FORT LEE, NEW JERSEY

Charleston  London

THE
History
PRESS

Published by The History Press
Charleston, SC 29403
www.historypress.net

First published 2011

Manufactured in the United States

ISBN 978.1.60949.456.8

Library of Congress Cataloging-in-Publication Data

Austin, Tom, 1939-
Bill Miller's Riviera : America's showplace in Fort Lee, New Jersey / Tom Austin and
Ron Kase.
p. cm.
Includes bibliographical references and index.
ISBN 978-1-60949-456-8
1. Riviera (Nightclub)--History. 2. Miller, Bill, 1904-2002. 3. Marden, Ben, d. 1973. 4.
Nightlife--New Jersey--Fort Lee--History--20th century. 5. Entertainers--New Jersey--Fort
Lee--History--20th century. 6. Fort Lee (N.J.)--Social life and customs--20th century. 7. Fort
Lee (N.J.)--Biography. 8. Fort Lee (N.J.)--History--20th century. I. Kase, Ron. II. Title.
F144.F67A97 2011
974.9'21--dc23
2011038706

Dedicated to the memory of the fathers: Al Austin and Gus Kase.

CONTENTS

ACKNOWLEDGEMENTS

The authors are indebted to the Fort Lee Film Commission (ftleefilm. org) and its executive director, Tom Meyers. The commission, founded in 2000, is dedicated to the recognition of Fort Lee, New Jersey, as the birthplace of the American motion picture industry. Tom Meyers—who has, for many years, promoted Fort Lee's history as having an important place in the American Revolution—founded the film commission and has led the organization to become the voice of Fort Lee's colorful past, a time when all of the nation's motion picture industry could be found on its streets.

Tom provided the authors with many of the rare photographs found in *Bill Miller's Riviera*, as well as advice and encouragement. He is Fort Lee's best booster and is a great supporter to anyone interested in the town's history. The authors and The History Press (the publisher) appreciate everything that Tom has done to make this book possible.

We also appreciate the assistance and support of Lou Azzolini, vice-president of the Fort Lee Historical Society (fortleehistoricalsociety.org).

Eric Nelsen, the historical interpreter for the Palisades Interstate Park Commission (mail@njpalisades.org), produced a wonderful history of the area that is available on a CD. Eric encouraged the writing of *Bill Miller's Riviera*, and for that the authors are grateful.

Of course, this book would not have been possible without the support of our very patient commissioning editor at The History Press, Whitney Tarella.

INTRODUCTION

Tom Austin grew up in Fort Lee, New Jersey, and Bill Miller's Riviera was a part of his life. Tom's father, Al Austin, worked at the Riviera and got to know many of the performers who headlined at the club. The big blue-and-yellow nightclub perched at the edge of the Palisades was a place of wonderment to Tom until his father, on occasion, would bring him to the club. Tom and his mother, a former band singer, had the unique opportunity of being allowed to see several of the Riviera's biggest shows on what were called "off nights" as guests of Bill Miller.

By the time Tom was a teenager, he was an accomplished drummer, having taken lessons from the Riviera's drummer, Irwin Russo. Tom played in several local bands and met keyboardist/composer Bob Gaudio (later of the *Jersey Boys*), and together they formed their own band, the Royal Teens. After collaborating on writing and recording two hits songs, "Short Shorts" and "Believe Me," they toured with Buddy Holly, Bill Haley and the Comets, Sam Cooke, Jackie Wilson, Jerry Lee Lewis and a host of others.

Tom, an artist of note, works in the mediums of oils and pen and inks. He has spent more than forty years as a real estate broker and was recently awarded the coveted designation of Realtor Emeritus.

Ron Kase grew up in Westchester County, New York. As a young boy sitting in the back of his father's Oldsmobile, he traveled along the Henry Hudson Parkway south to Manhattan's old West Side Highway. As they neared the George Washington Bridge, Kase could look out the car's window and see the mysterious blue-and-yellow structure on the cliff across the Hudson

River. He knew that Bill Miller's Riviera must have been a special place. Kase's parents had dinner there from time to time and hinted that they had entered the secret gambling casino upstairs in the Riviera.

Years later, after moving away from the area, Kase was disappointed to learn that the Riviera had disappeared sometime in the 1950s. He went on to a teaching career as a sociologist at New York City College of Technology (CUNY), an assistant provost and clinical professor at Fairleigh Dickinson University and an associate vice-president of Ramapo College of New Jersey. He is the author of the Fiddler Series of conspiracy novels (Behr) and *Images of America: Ramsey* (Arcadia).

The authors carefully researched the Riviera's intriguing story and were surprised about the large number of famous people who were involved in some way with the nightclub on the top of the Palisades. Many stories still remain to be told, and it's hoped that they will emerge when the book is distributed and read by those who remember the iconic place.

1919

THE YEAR JEAN RICHARD CREATED THE VILLA RICHARD

In an attempt to bring to life the social and economic atmosphere surrounding the story of "America's Showplace," the authors selected news stories from the year 1919 that examine the issues in which our society was involved.

The Bill Miller story is about American entertainment, so first we would like to point out that in 1919, the year when the Villa Richard was opened in Fort Lee, New Jersey, radio was just beginning. Silent movies provided the major source of entertainment. The most popular movie of 1919 was Cecil B. DeMille's *Male and Female*, starring Gloria Swanson.

Roller skating was sweeping across the country at the time. The craze was triggered by the Charlie Chaplin movie *The Rink*. Gramophone records were produced in mass quantity, replacing the outdated phonograph cylinders. Ballet, opera and symphonies were the sought-after tickets of the day, and sporting events such as boxing, baseball and horse racing were also very popular. Not everything was going in a positive direction, however. The United States was dealing with issues both political and social that share similarities with some of today's most serious events.

In 1919, the United States was in the grip of anarchist-inspired terrorist acts that were carried out by followers of Luigi Galleani. The Galleanists, as they became known, sent crude homemade bombs through the mail service to at least thirty prominent individuals on or near May 1, celebrated internationally by anarchists, communists and socialists as the day of revolutionary solidarity.

Most of the bomb packages were traced by the Post Office Department and defused, but some caused severe injuries to the addressees and their families. The list of addressees was impressive and included: John D. Rockefeller; Senator William King (Utah); Kenesaw Mountain Landis, U.S. district judge and later the first baseball commissioner; U.S. Attorney General A. Mitchell Palmer; J.P. Morgan; U.S. Supreme Court justice Oliver Wendell Homes Jr.; William C. Sproul, governor of Pennsylvania; and many others who had angered the Galleanists because of their actions concerning immigration. Another wave of violence was let loose against other judges, mayors and U.S. congressmen, some of whom were actually attacked in their homes. The rationalization for the violence was the Galleanists' desire "to rid the world of tyrannical institutions." They also claimed that "there will be blood shed, there will have to be murder, we will kill because it is necessary"—all uttered in the name of preserving humanity.

Following the first wave of violence, the Galleanists detonated one hundred pounds of dynamite on Wall Street in front of the J.P. Morgan & Company building, killing 38 bystanders and severely injuring 143 others. No one affiliated with J.P. Morgan was injured. The anarchists made sure that maximum human destruction would result from their act by adding five hundred pounds of lead window sash weights to the bomb, which caused most of the deaths and injuries.

In response to the deadly violence, U.S. Attorney General A. Mitchell Palmer organized a series of raids by police throughout the nation. The "Palmer Raids" arrested a mixture of thousands of violent radicals, "suspicious foreigners" and persons just caught up in the wide sweep of the raids during the period known as the Red Scare. A majority of Americans in 1919–20 believed that the United States government was in danger of being overthrown and that a Russian-style Bolshevist dictatorship would be put in place.

Once the Galleanists were arrested, tried, deported or jailed, the country got back to dealing with postwar issues. The First World War, or the Great War, was over, and the United States, Great Britain, France and Italy were trying to deal with Germany, Russia, Austria-Hungary and the Ottoman empire, all of which were no longer considered to be world powers. It was the greatest shifting of power since the collapse of the Roman empire. In order to ensure that the world would never again be engaged in a total war, the League of Nations was established, but the United States Senate would not approve membership for our nation even though President Woodrow Wilson was the force behind its establishment.

Americans were afraid that the League of Nations would replace national governments and that one world government would be established. Those fears persist today among a tiny minority of Americans who are opposed to the United Nations, the League's successor, which was established after World War II to end the threat of global war forever.

A significant event in 1919 was the death of President Theodore Roosevelt. He served two terms and attempted reelection after leaving the Republican Party. His Progressive Party, known as the Bull Moose Party, was defeated by William H. Taft. Roosevelt was New York's governor for only two years, but he created the Palisades Interstate Park in the Hudson Highlands region, which was being systematically ruined by rock quarrying along the magnificent New Jersey Palisades. Bill Miller's Riviera was among the last structures to be demolished as the Palisades Interstate Park Commission completed its land acquisition in 1953.

Roosevelt is best know as the commander of the Rough Riders, a volunteer cavalry that charged up Kettle Hill and San Juan Heights in Santiago, Cuba, in 1898 to help defeat the Spanish and end the Spanish-American War. Roosevelt and the Rough Riders—a group of cowboys, American Indians and college athletes who volunteered for the tough training—faced blistering heat and malaria in Cuba. They left from Tampa, Florida, on May 28, 1898, after dinner at the still popular Colombia Restaurant in Tampa's Ibor City section, which at the time was home to more than one hundred cigar factories.

Roosevelt, while president, turned 230 million acres of land into national parks and national forests. This monumental accomplishment took place decades before the terms "ecology," "environmentalism" or "sustainability" were a part of the language. Roosevelt had great vision, and he acted on it by putting the federal government squarely in the business of conservation. Theodore Roosevelt died at age sixty at his beloved Sagamore Hill home in Oyster Bay, New York.

The Spanish flu arrived in New York City late in 1918 as American soldiers returned home from the war in Europe. By 1919, an epidemic raged throughout the city and as far north as Buffalo, with pockets of influenza in Albany, Schenectady, Oswego and Syracuse, all in New York State. It was known as the Spanish flu because members of the Spanish royal family were suffering from it, as well as several million other Spaniards. Public health records were less than perfect in 1919, but it has been estimated that more than 50,000 deaths resulted from the flu in 1919 in New York and that more than 600,000 died in the United States. In total, about 50 million died throughout the world. It was the deadliest pandemic in modern history and the most deadly since the Black Death of the fourteenth century, which killed at least 450 million people in Europe.

The Spanish flu was caused by a virus, and even today we are not virus-proof. The disease attacked people between twenty and forty years old, which in itself was unusual since children and the elderly are typically the most vulnerable to flu. The nation was helpless, and the entire society felt the effects of the Spanish flu. All public gatherings were banned in New York City and Buffalo.

The 1990 film *Awakenings*, starring Robert De Niro and Robin Williams, was the depiction of a true story of a hospital ward in the Bronx filled with comatose patients who were victims of the 1919 Spanish flu. Williams, playing Dr. Oliver Sacks, treats the patients with a drug used to combat the effects of Parkinson's disease, and they respond by awakening after fifty years in a comatose state.

The mobster Al Capone wasn't a product of the Midwest, even though in 1919 he "owned Chicago." Capone was born in Brooklyn, New York, and later lived in peaceful Amityville, New York, on Long Island's south shore. Capone, a classic sociopath, suffered from syphilis, and in the time before the discovery of antibiotics, syphilis was often a death sentence, but first insanity usually overwhelmed the patient.

The south shore of Long Island was the main point of entry into the United States for illegal whiskey. Capone had been involved in bootlegging since he was a teenager, and at twenty he was wealthy and well known. He moved to Chicago and, through murders and massacres, took complete control of all major crime in the Midwest. In spite of Capone's bloody hands, he was welcome to contribute to various charitable events in Chicago and was seen by some misguided people as a folk hero. During a long prison term for tax evasion, his only conviction, his syphilis became full blown, and he became delusional. Capone remained in very poor health until his death in 1947 from natural causes.

Writers from Damon Runyon to F. Scott Fitzgerald to Jimmy Breslin—who have used New York City as the background for their stories, filled with colorful characters in or near the city's underworld—have frequently used the real-life character Arnold Rothstein as a model. Rothstein was born in 1892 and lived only forty-six years. He was shot in the Park Central Hotel in Manhattan and died the next day. The shooting of Rothstein, who was usually surrounded by body guards, was revenge for his not paying a $320,000 debt incurred during a three-day poker game.

Rothstein was at the top of the Jewish mafia, along with Meyer Lansky, and was closely connected to Charles "Lucky" Luciano, the head of the Sicilian-American mafia. Lansky and Luciano remained close friends and business associates for their entire lives and had their last partnership in Cuba's casinos and radio stations in the 1960s.

Rothstein was known as a gambler, and it was alleged that he actually fixed the 1919 World Series. This was the darkest time in Major League Baseball's glorious history. Apparently, Rothstein paid members of the Chicago White Sox to throw the World Series games played against the Cincinnati Reds. The Reds won, and Rothstein, who had bet on them, made at least $1 million. Even before the series had begun, there were rumors among gamblers that Rothstein had it fixed and that Cincinnati would win. The open discussion of the fix didn't deter the baseball commissioner, Judge Kenesaw Mountain Landis, from allowing the series to go on unimpeded, but after it was over Landis acted swiftly. Eight White Sox players were permanently suspended from playing baseball, including the very popular "Shoeless Joe" Jackson, even though his participation is still in dispute. Charles Cominsky, owner of the White Sox, was blamed by some insiders because Cominsky was known to be cheap when it came to paying his players, and they wanted to teach him a lesson.

What became known as the Black Sox Scandal was only one of a list of audacious acts by Rothstein, who was a public figure, with his "office" in the famed Lindy's Restaurant on Broadway, known for its cheesecake. He usually could be found there every day with bodyguards, collecting and paying gambling debts—just like the characters in *Guys and Dolls*, Damon Runyon's portrayal of the New York gambling scene in the 1930s. Rothstein even conspired to fix the Travers Stakes run each August at the iconic Saratoga Race Course in Saratoga Springs, New York, where illegal gambling casinos controlled by Meyer Lansky flourished in public for decades. The Travers, the oldest thoroughbred stake race in the country, wasn't immune to Rothstein's machinations. Rothstein won more than $500,000 from betting on the Travers in 1921 during the August racing season in Saratoga Springs.

Rothstein is a permanent part of the popular culture. He was portrayed as Meyer Wolfsheim in the 1973 film *The Great Gatsby*, starring Robert Redford and Mia Farrow. He was the inspiration for the pool game between "Minnesota Fats" and "Fast Eddie" Felson in *The Hustler*. He is mentioned in the films *The Godfather Part II*, *Eight Men Out* and *The Big Bankroll* (also known as *King of the Roaring 20's*). Currently, in the HBO series *Boardwalk Empire*, Rothstein is played by Michael Stuhlbarg.

The year 1919 saw the beginning of the lunch meetings of the Algonquin Round Table in the Algonquin Hotel on Manhattan's West Forty-fourth Street. It is the oldest operating hotel in New York City and a national landmark. Hotel owner Frank Case closed the Algonquin's bar in 1919 and was an outspoken critic of those who operated speakeasies.

The Algonquin Round Table consisted of a group of intellectuals from journalism and publishing, writers, critics and stage directors, as well as a few others, who met most weekdays for lunch in the Algonquin's Rose Room. This was the most outspoken and intellectually powerful group of its time. The members set the tone for literary discussion in New York's intellectual circles. While they were referred to in the press as the Algonquin Round Table, they called themselves the "Vicious Circle." The Round Table met from 1919 to 1929 and included Robert Benchley, Dorothy Parker, Marc Connelly, Deems Taylor, George S. Kaufman, Harpo Marx, Alexander Woollcott, Edna Ferber, Heywood Broun and Frank Crowninshield. The members became important figures in their fields, and many of the tales about them originated from the Algonquin Round Table.

Other events in the 1919 worth remembering are the founding of the Hilton Hotel chain by Conrad Hilton in Cisco, Texas; the popular musical hits "Alice Blue Gown," "Dardanella," "I Wish I Could Shimmy Like My Sister Kate," "I'm Forever Blowing Bubbles," "Irene," "Let the Rest of the World Go By," "A Pretty Girl Is Like A Melody," "Swanee," "The World Is Waiting for the Sunrise" and "Baby, Won't You Please Come Home?"

The Hotel Pennsylvania opened on January 25, 1919, built by the Pennsylvania Railroad and operated by Statler Hotels, which were later merged into the Hilton Hotel chain. The Pennsylvania was designed by the architectural firm McKim, Mead and White, which also designed the beautiful Pennsylvania Railroad Station directly across from the hotel. The hotel has the broadest sidewalk set back in New York City and could be also accessed from a tunnel that ran below the street from Pennsylvania Station. The station was one of the largest indoor spaces in the world. In 1963, the Pennsylvania Station was razed in order to build a new Madison Square Garden. Historians, architects and preservationists have mourned the destruction of what was a brilliant example of a Roman-inspired Doric temple to transportation.

The Pennsylvania Station and Pennsylvania Hotel had their own telephone exchange, Pennsylvania 6, made famous by the Glen Miller Orchestra's rendition of "Pennsylvania 6-5000," the 1940 top five *Billboard* hit. Glen Miller and many other famous orchestras played the Hotel Pennsylvania's Café Rouge Ballroom.

Births in 1919 included that of Nat King Cole, Don Cornell, Pete Seeger, Liberace, Marge and Gower Champion (who appeared regularly at Bill Miller's Riviera), George Shearing, Art Blakey and Anita O'Day. All became prominent performers and had long careers.

AMERICA'S SHOWPLACE

There was a time known as the Roaring Twenties, when the Charleston and the Black Bottom were the dance crazes of the day and women called "flappers" wore short skirts and cloche hats. Whiskey was "hootch," nightclubs serving illegal whiskey were called "speakeasies" and illegal gambling casinos had an electric atmosphere attracting players who craved the action. In this swirling society, two men emerged who became well known by the famous and the infamous who were connected with show business and night life. They were Ben Marden and Bill Miller. What they shared, besides their initials, was the dream of owning the greatest nightclub in America.

Nightclubs, as places to be seen and entertained, gained great popularity beginning in the late 1920s. The growth was partially due to the influence of the black-and-white movies produced by the motion picture industry—first in Fort Lee, New Jersey, and later in Hollywood—that showed stylish people enjoying champagne, sophisticated dialogue and elaborate musical numbers featuring big bands, popular singers, stunning chorus lines and famous dancers. The motion pictures set the stage for the elaborate nightclubs that opened in major cities, with New York offering the most clubs in number and elegance. The leading New York clubs included the El Morocco, Tropicana, Sherman Billingsly's Stork Club, Lou Walters's Latin Quarter (he was TV's Barbara Walters's father) and Jules Podell's Copacabana. In addition, New York's famous hotels, including the Astor, Waldorf-Astoria, the Roosevelt, the Hotel Pennsylvania and the Plaza, hosted clubs and ballrooms that featured big bands. New York was the place for sophisticated night life, which was duly reported in the gossip columns of

The original Villa Richard hotel that became the first Riviera. *Courtesy of the Fort Lee Historical Society.*

the city's ten daily newspapers. Individuals and show business personalities hired press agents to get their names in the columns written by Walter Winchell, Westbrook Pegler, Ed Sullivan, Earl Wilson and the *Journal-American's* top gossiper, Dorothy Kilgallen. A mention in a column by one of the city's powerful newspaper writers was priceless for promoting careers in show business, politics or "café society." On the other hand, a "knock" in a New York newspaper column could disrupt lives and careers quicker than a tornado. Before they were national headlines, scandals involving sex and crime were often noted by the columnists, who roved the New York nights from club to club seeking tidbits for the next day's publication.

The 1957 motion picture *Sweet Smell of Success* starred Burt Lancaster as the tough, bullying newspaper columnist J.J. Hunsecker who, because of his nationally syndicated daily column, always got his way. The Clifford Odets story, while fiction, was loosely based on the lives of columnists Walter Winchell, who also had a radio show, and Westbrook Pegler. Both men were known for their lack of compassion and demanding manner. On the West Coast, Hedda Hopper was the exalted queen of the Hollywood gossip columnists; it was said that she exercised more power in her ten-inch newspaper column than any head of a major motion picture studio.

New York's nightclubs operated every night but Sunday. There were scenes of love and lust, drama and passion, triumph and failure played out daily among the expensively clad audience—sometimes also including the famous performers as well. Almost all of the city's noted nightclubs were found in the central part of Manhattan. The exception was the Cotton Club, originally located on 142nd Street and Lenox Avenue in Harlem, which was owned first by Ben Marden and then by the bootlegger Owney Madden. It was one of the only fashionable clubs uptown. The Cotton Club was unique because it hired only black waiters, bartenders and hatcheck and cigarette girls and featured only black entertainers; however, the clientele was all white. Madden, a notorious gangster, bought the Cotton Club from Ben Marden while Madden was serving a term in Sing Sing prison. Madden was so powerful that he arranged to have the Cotton Club's chorus girls perform on the stage in Sing Sing to entertain the inmates.

However, New York's most famous nightclub wasn't in New York at all. It was located across the Hudson River opposite Manhattan's 182nd Street, in Fort Lee, New Jersey. The club was the iconic Riviera, known as America's Showplace, and it set the standard for nightclubs and later influenced the development of the entertainment offered by Las Vegas's fledging hotel industry.

The Riviera opened in 1931 on top of the beautiful rock formations known as the Palisades. The nightclub was close to the New Jersey entrance to the George Washington Bridge, built in 1931, which connected New York City with Fort Lee, New Jersey. The bridge changed the sleepy rural communities of northern New Jersey into dynamic suburbs of Manhattan. Before the bridge's construction, the only direct automobile route from Manhattan to New Jersey was through the Holland Tunnel, opened in 1927. The tunnel connected a run-down part of New York City to an even more run-down area of Jersey City. Ferryboats operated from several terminals in Manhattan and on the New Jersey side of the river, bringing passengers across the busy waterway.

The Riviera was first known as Ben Marden's, named for the show business entrepreneur who built the fanciful nightclub that was actually perched at the edge of the Palisades atop the ancient rock cliffs rising hundreds of feet from the bank of the Hudson River. The entire twenty-one miles of the Palisades was designated a national historical landmark in 1986. It's a world-class tourist attraction best viewed from a Circle Line tour boat on the river.

While motion pictures produced in the 1920s and '30s were stimuli for the popularity of nightclubs and other chic places known as supper clubs, the underlying reason for clubbing and the existence of café society was the failed institution known as prohibition. Under mounting pressure

The Marine Terrace of Ben Marden's Riviera. *Courtesy of the Fort Lee Historical Society.*

from the Women's Christian Temperance Union (WCTU) and the Anti-Saloon League, the United States Congress in 1919 passed the Eighteenth Amendment to the U.S. Constitution, prohibiting the manufacture, sale or transportation of intoxicating liquor. Interesting enough, the consumption of alcohol was not made illegal. Later in 1919, the Volstead Act was passed to administer and criminalize the effects of the Eighteenth Amendment. The results of this experiment in social engineering were the establishment of organized crime in America and the ushering in of the Roaring Twenties.

Centered in Chicago and led by the notorious Al Capone, organized crime families controlled alcohol distilleries in Canada, Mexico and the Caribbean, where it was legal to produce whiskey. The alcohol was moved by trucks from Canada over back roads and by boat to secret coves in Florida and New Orleans. The whiskey finally reached shuttered clubs, where stylish people congregated, rubbing elbows with gangsters and fancy call girls. The lure of illegal liquor was strong, and music, dance and fashion mirrored the excitement of the time. Flappers—women who dressed in revealing clothing, smoked and drank whiskey in public and had their hair cut short or bobbed—were fixtures in upscale speakeasies, where the music was loud and liquor flowed until it was raided and shut down by federal agents; it only opened again soon thereafter in another place. Speakeasies were found everywhere. Most were modest establishments in ordinary neighborhoods. Some others in New York and Chicago were elegant places where patrons

The lobby of Ben Marden's first Riviera. *Courtesy of the Fort Lee Historical Society.*

drank whiskey in China teacups and socialized with senators and the local police commissioner.

Prohibition continued as a largely ignored law until the Twenty-first Amendment, passed in 1933, repealed the Eighteenth Amendment, the first and only constitutional amendment ever repealed. With liquor legal again, organized crime, now entrenched in America's Northeast and the industrialized cities of the Midwest, turned to other profitable pursuits. The speakeasies became clubs and restaurants, still catering to the smart set, and were often secretly owned by mob associates with a real restaurateur as the public face. Jack & Charley's 21 Club on New York's Fifty-second Street is one of the city's most well-known restaurants that made the transition from prohibition speakeasy to elegant bistro.

Ben Marden, who successfully operated nightclubs in Florida and Manhattan, found a small hotel for sale just north of Fort Lee, New Jersey, at the eastern end of Myrtle Avenue. The Villa Richard (pronounced "ri-*chard*") was owned by Jean Richard, former chef of Delmonico's, a landmark restaurant in Manhattan. Delmonico's was owned by Edward L.C. Robbins and catered to New York's Four Hundred, as the city's wealthiest families were known. The restaurant also attracted the moviemakers D.W. Griffith, Lillian Gish, Mary Pickford, Charlie Chaplin, Pearl White and many others who were regular customers while they made movies in Fort Lee, New

Jersey. The little town of Fort Lee was home to the major studios of the day, including Biograph, Peerless-World, Fox and Éclair. The movie folk gave Chef Richard the confidence he needed to strike out on his own as a hotelier and restaurateur when Delmonico's closed in 1919 due to the effects of prohibition. Jean Richard took a chance and opened up a hotel and restaurant on Hudson Terrace in Coytesville in the borough of Fort Lee, away from the prying eyes of the law. He could serve his customers food and drink in the manner to which they were accustomed. It's likely that some of Jean Richard's best patrons from Delmonico's became the investors that made Villa Richard possible.

The Villa Richard was a Mediterranean-style hotel with a restaurant, and it survived the Prohibition era by offering first-class whiskey distilled in Canada, along with fine cuisine similar to Delmonico's. The Villa flourished until the motion picture industry began to move across the country to Hollywood in California. Attracted by the mild weather, huge outdoor spaces and cheap land for building the sprawling studios, the motion picture companies abandoned Fort Lee and the East. By 1930, the movie industry was gone and the Villa Richard was boarded up.

A year later, Ben Marden—the owner of record of the Colonial Inn in Hallandale, Florida, a chic gambling house—bought the Villa Richard and renovated the entire building, turning it into a top nightclub, which he named

The grand dining room of Ben Marden's first Riviera. *Courtesy of the Fort Lee Historical Society.*

the Riviera. It quickly became popular with New Yorkers, who traveled across the new George Washington Bridge in limousines after paying the toll of twenty-five cents per car. The club was wildly successful and became the favorite place of politicians, gangsters and prominent business leaders, whose interests often ran together—and all wanted to avoid the spotlight of the Manhattan night spots because of whom they were with or with whom they left. The original Riviera featured famous bands like the Paul Whitman Orchestra, and even Bing Crosby once sang there.

Ben Marden's Riviera had five good years of flowing liquor, chorus lines, celebrities and profits, but in November 1936 on Thanksgiving night, it burned down, leaving nothing but memories. At first, Marden was devastated. He had only minimum insurance on the building, but almost miraculously during the middle of America's Great Depression, he raised $250,000, roughly equivalent to $4 million in 2010. With this windfall, Marden set about designing and constructing a new Riviera that would look and feel like no other nightclub in the world. He succeeded, and a great Art Deco yellow-and-blue building rose on the top of the Palisades, where no other structure will ever be built. The Riviera's iconic design resembled a grand yacht. Its curving front close to the cliff's edge turned slightly toward the bridge, sporting huge windows that looked out at the massive suspension bridge that was an engineering marvel for its time. On warm nights, the windows were lowered into the floor by electric motors and the roof opened so that patrons had the illusion of dining and dancing out of doors while enjoying the music of two orchestras alternating on a revolving bandstand. The dance floor also revolved, adding to the feeling of being in a magical place. Up to 1,200 diners filled the huge dining room, with an additional 200 or so in the bar area on nights that featured top-flight performers. Show business legends Frank Sinatra, Lena Horne, Tony Martin, Vic Damone, Jackie Gleason and dozens of other headliners regularly appeared at the Riviera.

While most patrons enjoyed the fine cuisine, the music and the shows on the main floor, a select clientele found its way up a hidden stairway that led to a secret floor that could not be seen if one was looking at the outside of the building. The "secret," which everyone seemed to know about, was the full gambling casino located upstairs in the Riviera where dice were thrown, cards dealt, wheels spun and slot machine handles pulled until the early hours of the morning. Marden's silent Riviera partners, some from his former business in Florida, were experienced gambling operators and welcomed the opportunity to work outside the scrutiny of New York City's political establishment in order to ensure that the casino's continuous operation was undisturbed by New Jersey and federal anti-gambling laws.

The Riviera closed during World War II. Food rationing, the army draft and scarce gasoline for automobiles made it impossible to continue operations. When it reopened in 1946, it had a new sign and a new owner. Broadway talent agent Bill Miller bought the Riviera from Ben Marden for an undisclosed sum, which some have guessed was about $750,000 (equivalent to $9,585,000 today), a princely sum for a talent agent to pay out, even one as successful as Miller. The transaction fed the rumor that Miller had partners who didn't want to be publicly identified. Abner "Longy" Zwillman and Willie Moretti were the two most often mentioned, but only quietly, since both were notorious gangsters accused of murder and extortion. Miller continued the policy of booking first-rate talent that was often seen by 2,500 people during two Riviera shows on weekend nights. He introduced Sammy Davis Jr., along with his father and uncle. They performed as the Will Masten Trio until Davis was launched nationally by Ed Sullivan on his long-running Sunday night television show after seeing the trio at the Riviera. Dean Martin appeared at the Riviera before teaming up with Jerry Lewis. Jack Carter, the Ames Brothers, Milton Berle, Martha Ray and Zero Mostel appeared there before their successful television careers.

The Riviera flourished during one of America's most stressful economic periods. The Great Depression, which spanned the decade between 1929 and 1940, saw an economic turndown for the United States and eventually the rest of the world. In the United States, unemployment rose to 25 percent, and inflation followed. A severe drought continuing over several years in the mid-1930s, turned much of the Midwest and Southwest into dust bowls, which led to bank foreclosures and the abandoning of thousands of farms.

The Roaring Twenties and the Jazz Age were over. Large, complex social programs funded by the federal government provided work. The Social Security Act began to provide a social safety net for the working class. New legislation regulated the stock market and banks, promoted union activity and evaluated food and drugs, and subsequently industrial safety laws were passed. World War II ended, and a new era of postwar prosperity began. Bill Miller's Riviera was a symbol for letting the good times roll once again, which continued until the club was closed in October 1953 due to the expansion of the Palisades Interstate Parkway.

1931
THE YEAR BEN MARDEN OPENED THE RIVIERA

The Hudson River Bridge was completed in 1931, perhaps the year's most significant event. When the bridge opened to automobile traffic on October 25, 1931, it was the longest suspension bridge in the world, but that designation was soon lost as other, longer bridges were built. The bridge's name was changed a year before it was completed to the George Washington Memorial Bridge. Sometime later, the name was shortened to the George Washington Bridge.

Legendary architect Le Corbusier wrote with enthusiasm about the bridge: "The George Washington Bridge over the Hudson is the most beautiful bridge in the world. Made of cables and steel beams, it gleams in the sky like a reversed arch. It is blessed. It is the only seat of grace in the disoriented city."

As early as 1906, the governors of New York and New Jersey proposed the construction of a bridge between Manhattan and New Jersey. Gustav Lindenthal, a genius of a bridge builder, supported building a trans-Hudson bridge from midtown Manhattan to New Jersey. There was great interest from the business community on both sides of the river in Lindenthal's plan. Engineer and bridge builder Othmar Ammann disagreed with Lindenthal's proposal and persuaded New Jersey's governor and the newly formed Port Authority to construct the bridge between Washington Heights in the north end of Manhattan and Fort Lee, New Jersey. Ammann was given the go-ahead in 1925 to design the bridge. He hired renowned architect Cass Gilbert to provide design assistance. Gilbert was the designer of the landmark Woolworth Building on Manhattan's lower Broadway. The building is still one of New York's architectural treasures.

America's Showplace in Fort Lee, New Jersey

The original design included commuter railroad tracks, which were abandoned early in the design phase. The final design was a great challenge since the 3,500-foot spans would be twice as long as any existing suspension bridge. Ammann overcame this and engineered the bridge so that it didn't sway even in the strongest wind storms. A lower deck was added in 1959 that was actually anticipated in Ammann's design.

Significantly, the bridge opened up northeastern New Jersey and made Fort Lee a place of importance to the point that the Riviera nightclub that became America's Showplace was opened in 1931 less than half a mile from the bridge's Fort Lee entrance. The second Riviera, the splendid Art Deco structure built on the Palisades, was one hundred yards from the bridge; the fantastic views of the bridge were part of its appeal.

The bridge was finished and ready for automobile traffic eight months ahead of schedule. It cost $59 million, and twelve construction workers lost their lives during its construction. Governor Franklin D. Roosevelt of New York and Governor Morgan F. Larsen of New Jersey stood side by side and dedicated the bridge on October 25, 1931, to George Washington with more than thirty thousand attending the ceremony.

The City Beautiful movement of the early 1900s had an influence on the design of the bridge's plazas. There were plans for landscaping and fountains at the places that cars entered and exited the George Washington Bridge. Unfortunately, the predicted high-speed traffic and its high volume made it necessary to construct instead a series of ramps to move the traffic along efficiently. Neither the Manhattan nor the Fort Lee access roads can qualify as attractive places.

The unemployment rate in 1931 was an astounding 16.3 percent, which was still a result of the 1929 stock market crash. The nation was having a difficult time regaining financial stability. Unemployment insurance, widely used at present, was unknown in 1931. Until the passage of the Social Security Act in 1935, the federal government did not support weekly payments in lieu of salaries. There was a limited program of relief payments made from 1929 to 1935, but the Social Security Act institutionalized unemployment compensation in all of the states. In 1931, a gallon of gasoline cost ten cents, bread eight cents and a pound of hamburger eleven cents, but the average wage per year for those who were employed was $1,850.

The Empire State Building opened in 1931 and was the world's tallest building for forty years. It was built during the Great Depression on Fifth Avenue and Thirty-fourth Street in Manhattan, away from all of the city's transportation centers. The beautiful Art Deco–styled structure struggled for several years to attract tenants for its spacious office floors. The Chemical Bank & Trust Company opened its largest branch on the lobby floor, and Longchamps Restaurants operated a multileveled, ultra chic eating place off the lobby along Thirty-third Street.

The Empire State Building Corporation was headed by Alfred E. Smith, the former governor of New York and recent candidate for president. Smith, the first Catholic to run for president, lost to Herbert Hoover. The Empire State Building remains one of New York's major attractions. Its observation decks have attracted millions of visitors since they opened, and currently a $550 million renovation is ongoing to restore the Art Deco aspects of the building's public areas. The Empire State Building was featured in several major motion pictures: *An Affair to Remember* (1957), *Love Affair* (1939 and 1994 versions), *Sleepless in Seattle* (1993), *Empire* (Andy Warhol's eight hour silent film from 1964) and, of course, the most memorable, *King Kong* (1933 and 2005 versions).

In 1931, the State of Nevada passed a law that permitted all types of gambling to be offered in the state. This opened up Nevada for development of legal gambling, now known as gaming, for the first time in modern American history. It took almost twenty years before the local Nevada casinos were eclipsed by the new hotel-casinos secretly owned or controlled by mob people from around the nation.

Vincent "Mad Dog" Coll, an Irish-born New York gangster, conducted a reign of terror in 1931. The vicious criminal attacked anyone in his way, including rival gangsters and innocent bystanders. The sociopath Coll just didn't care. In 1931, he kidnapped radio personality Rudy Vallee, for whom a ransom of $100,000 was paid. Next he kidnapped Sherman Billingsley, owner of the Stork Club, New York's most exclusive supper club. Coll was so fearless that he also kidnapped members of other gangs and collected ransoms for them. Dutch Schultz, another infamous mobster with several murders to his credit, posted a $50,000 reward for killing Coll. The reward was collected after a member of bootlegger Owney Madden's gang fired eighteen bullets into a phone booth that Coll was using.

The year 1931 passed into history, leaving a legacy of intertwined events that combined well-known criminals with equally well-known figures in show business and public life. The famous mobsters who were celebrities in their own right added to the colorful period because the public found them exciting and the news media often painted them as merely scoundrels rather than coldblooded murderers. Somehow Ben Marden, by all reports a gentleman, was able to coexist with the gangsters and not be affected by their violent way of life.

BEN MARDEN

B en Marden was known as a man who could do many things at one time. Today he would be called a multitasker. Although he is most recognized as the one who built Ben Marden's Riviera on the New Jersey side of the Hudson, his nightclubs and other investments reached from New York and New Jersey to Florida and even to Cuba. Marden's involvement with nightclubs began in Hallandale, Florida, where he was an owner in the Colonial Inn, an upscale showplace and supper club that was the cover for a major gambling casino. History logs his silent partners in that adventure as the ubiquitous Meyer Lansky, along with Lansky's brother, Jake, and a plethora of other underworld figures. Lansky, known as the "mob's accountant," was trusted by America's crime syndicate figures with their money, which Lansky "washed" through his Miami National Bank and, later on, through a Swiss bank that Lansky actually set up and operated from Miami.

New York, however, was the most sought-after place for Ben and his partners. They knew that they would profit in the fast-moving environment that surrounded chic clubs that attracted the era's beautiful people. It didn't take long before Ben opened up a nightclub called the Palais Royale located on West Forty-eighth Street, where the Latin Quarter eventually stood. The Palais Royale presented the city's most extravagant shows and friendliest showgirls. They adorned the stage and were considered New York's most gorgeous "chorines," as they were called—their beautiful and elegant (though skimpy) costumes inflamed the imagination. The club's lavish stage shows and reviews impressed the New York critics into inventing new words like "stupendous" and "boffo." Although it appeared that Ben was "knocking

Sophie Tucker, the "Red Hot Mama," explains "What a little lovin' can do." *Courtesy of the Fort Lee Historical Society.*

'em dead on 48th Street," according to the columnists, the action was not the same as the making of huge profits from gambling at the Colonial Inn in Hallandale, where the odds were always in favor of the house. Marden also opened up the famed Cotton Club in Manhattan's Harlem section.

Something better did come along in the late 1920s when word leaked out that the political leaders in New York and New Jersey had decided to link the two states with a mile-long suspension bridge. It became valuable to know where the bridge was going to be located and who owned the property adjacent to that place—property that could be obtained early, before the news of the planned bridge was made public. Ben and his investors hopped the ferry across the Hudson and made their way up the cliffs in Fort Lee to seek and obtain property in a place that would allow them to operate in relative comfort outside the scrutiny of New York's officials—such a gambling club that attracted huge crowds of patrons would not have gone unnoticed.

The earliest planning stages for the George Washington Bridge, of course, had taken place years before the official groundbreaking date of October

Right: Sophie and Ben Marden have a laugh. *Courtesy of the Fort Lee Historical Society.*

Below: The original Riviera, with the future George Washington Bridge superimposed. *Courtesy of the Fort Lee Historical Society.*

Ben Marden's "RIVIERA" ON THE HUDSON FORT LEE N.J. Show Place of the World

1927. The politicians representing both states must have spent countless hours mulling over who was going to have jurisdiction over the bridge; it was actually ceded to the Port Authority of New York, founded in 1921 and later renamed the Port Authority of New York and New Jersey. Some gamblers never depend on luck as their catalyst for anteing up their chips, and for Ben and his investors to consider buying an old wooden hotel built in 1901 in a remote place with limited access for New Yorkers, it seemed far-fetched. Fort Lee, New Jersey, in the 1920s was a place where dogs ran free and the residents hunted in the woods; it was a community where the movie industry was dying and not much else was happening. It wasn't the kind of place to which smart investors would look to invest their cash unless their uncanny intuition told them that something would happen there that the uninformed public did not know. Ben Marden acquired the Villa Richard, an old hotel and restaurant, in 1931, the same year the bridge opened, and immediately invested $100,000 to spruce up the place in order to attract a sophisticated crowd. One can speculate that Ben and his negotiators did a masterful job of somehow convincing Chef Richard to sell the Villa Richard at the most opportune time, the opening of the George Washington Bridge.

By the time Swiss-born engineer Othmar H. Ammann, working for the Port Authority, completed his design work and the bridge construction was finished in 1931, Ben had already renovated the Villa. When he was ready to open the doors for business in his new place—with its new name, Ben Marden's Riviera, in huge rooftop letters flashing across the New Jersey skyline—the larders was fully stocked with the finest Canadian whiskey and choice beef that money could buy and connections could get, and his entertainment was the best of the day. Ben stacked the deck when he booked Sophie Tucker, Harry Richman and Joe E. Lewis to appear in the same show, thus telling the world that he was open for business in New Jersey. The demographics of the time indicated that older, wealthier club attendees would have enjoyed the Riviera's shows. Obviously money was no object, and Ben hired the most popular stars of the day. By today's standards, it could be compared to booking Bruce Springsteen, Bon Jovi and Elton John to all appear in the same show. It wasn't long before New York's powerful gossip columnists were flocking to the Riviera to see who and what was causing all the excitement.

Just imagine Sophie Tucker, the aging sex symbol, arriving in her new chauffer-driven Hispano Suiza automobile up Hudson Terrace to greet her adoring fans. Hispano Suiza automobiles were manufactured by a Spanish-Swiss company. Sophie first saw a Hispano Suiza owned by moviemaker

D.W. Griffith. The model he owned was a six-cylinder, Victoria town car, manufactured in Barcelona, Spain. It had six wheels, four in the back and two in the front. Sophie immediately fell in love with the car and sought to purchase one. When she found out that they were not readily available and would have to wait at least a year for delivery, she set about trying to find someone who owned one and might be willing to sell it to her. Sophie's research led her to a gentleman. It took only one week for Sophie to convince her admirer to give the car to her. After he completed his gifting, she gave him one last thank-you over a long weekend and dumped him—of course, she kept the car. Sophie's attraction to nightclub audiences was her off-color stage dialogue uttered during a period of heavy censorship of everything sexual. Local, state and federal laws strictly controlled sexual representations of any manner until 1967, when the U.S. Supreme Court struck down laws that prohibited adults from reading, hearing or seeing sexually explicit material.

The 1950 motion picture *Sunset Boulevard*, starring Gloria Swanson as the disoriented, former silent film star Norma Desmond, featured another classic

Waiter captains and doormen await the arrival of patrons at the new Ben Marden's Riviera. *Courtesy of the Fort Lee Historical Society.*

automobile, a 1929 Isotta-Fraschini Tipo 8A Castagna, which was driven in the movie by the great early film director Erich von Stroheim playing the role of Miss Desmond's chauffer. The Isotta-Fraschini was used in the film after negations for renting the Victoria formally owned by D.W. Griffith broke down over the fee, which was said to be $50,000. Gloria Swanson's magnificent estate, called Gloria Crest in Englewood Cliffs, is a neo–Beverly Hills movie star's compound that features an imposing white Mediterranean mansion built in the 1920s. Gloria Crest, which is still a beautiful property today, is located less than a mile from Ben Marden's original Riviera.

Marden was listed as the owner of the Colonial Inn in Florida and did oversee the entertainment and restaurant operations. The actual owner was Meyer Lansky, who controlled gambling at the Colonial, as well as in Saratoga Springs, New York; Miami; New Orleans; and later in Las Vegas and Cuba. His partner and Lansky's sponsor into the depths of the Italian crime syndicate known as the La Costa Nostra was Charles "Lucky" Luciano, the nation's most notorious gangster, who was responsible for creating the National Crime Syndicate and the five mafia families of New York City. Luciano and Lansky were childhood friends, along with Arnold Rothstein. They grew up on the Lower East Side of Manhattan in poverty and on the streets. Rothstein was shot and killed over a gambling debt in 1928. Lansky and Luciano forged a lifetime bond to protect each other and split the profits from the huge web of businesses, both criminal and legitimate, that Lansky controlled. Luciano realized that crime, if organized like a business, would be more successful than random mayhem. Lansky, an organizational genius who could have rivaled General Electric's former chairman Jack Welsh, ran an illegal empire that Lansky proclaimed in 1951 to be "bigger than U.S. Steel."

Lansky, always ready to bring in partners to share his ventures, which was the secret of his success and longevity, encouraged New Jersey mobster Willie Moretti, who had interests in several gambling casinos, to become involved with Marden and the Riviera. Moretti, whose gambling spots in the Garden State featured local singers and dancers, had heard a young crooner from Hoboken named Frank Sinatra, and he was impressed with the slight young man. Moretti took him under his wing, hiring him to perform at his casinos and at Ben Marden's Riviera. Sinatra soon became a regular at another showplace, the Rustic Cabin in Englewood Cliffs, a short distance from the Riviera, where a local radio station broadcast his live performances. Sinatra continued to perform at the original Riviera and later at Bill Miller's. He began his musical comeback there after starring in the film *From Here to Eternity*.

Names like Paul Whiteman and his orchestra and Bing Crosby were only two of the innumerable top talents that graced the stage of Ben Marden's Riviera. Sophisticated couples like Joan Crawford and Franchot Tone, two of the most popular movie stars of the day, also frequented the club. In 1935, Crawford and Tone married in Fort Lee. Documentation states that the mayor of Fort Lee at the time performed the ceremony; local information states that they were also married in a ceremony at the Dutch Reformed Church of the Palisades on Lemoine Avenue, only four blocks away from the Riviera. Reverend Kelder performed their wedding. Maybe Franchot wanted to be married by the mayor, and perhaps Joan wanted to be married in the church, so they did both. The luster for the glamorous couple wore off in 1939 when they were divorced. Joan stated at that time that if she ever talked of marriage again "someone should punch me in the jaw."

The Riviera's immediate success, accompanied by the public illumination it created, must have bothered some of the good people of New Jersey, as Marden fell from their grace. It wasn't long before the honeymoon time was over, and Bergen County detectives raided his establishment and confiscated more than 150 cases of whiskey and wine, which were then, of course, used for medicinal purposes. The harassment continued until December 5, 1933, when the ratification of the Twenty-first Amendment repealed the Eighteenth Amendment, thus ending prohibition. However, United States federal law still prohibited the manufacture of distilled spirits without meeting numerous licensing requirements, which made it impractical to produce alcohol for personal beverage use. Tell that to all of the Italian families who moved to Fort Lee after immigrating to the United States because they were needed as stonemasons for the building of the George Washington Bridge. Vineyards were springing up everywhere in Fort Lee, as Italians crushed their own grapes and made their own wine in their backyards.

Ben Marden was a very generous man to everyone with whom he came into contact. It was his custom to prepare more than five hundred food baskets every Thanksgiving for families who were having a hard time due to the depression that still gripped the nation. It was after the cook staff had prepared the food baskets in the Riviera's kitchen on November 25, 1936, that the old wooden structure caught fire and burned to the ground during the middle of the night.

The following day, the *Bergen Record* ran the story that all that was left of the Riviera was a pile of smoldering ruins. Fire Chief Frank Schmidt sought the cause of the fire, which had spread so quickly that four Fort Lee fire companies, reinforced by two from Englwood Cliffs, could do little to douse the flames. The story went on to say that only 10 percent of the building was covered by insurance. John Tierney, a Fort Lee fireman, was overcome by ammonia fumes when the resort's refrigerating plant exploded.

Ironically, it must have been extreme farsightedness on the part of Ben Marden that he had already acquired land one-quarter mile south of the old Riviera on a far superior site, much closer to the George Washington Bridge. This place would make a much better location for a new Riviera. After the new building was constructed, from elaborate plans developed by Marden and architect Louis Allen Abramson, the huge neon sign that was erected over the nightclub read Ben Marden's Riviera, and a new era of the Riviera legend began.

Marden had grown weary of the café business in New Jersey. Like many New Yorkers of a certain age and economic status, Ben was attracted to Cuba, only ninety miles over the sea from Key West, Florida. For several years, during the winter months when the Riviera was closed, he operated the casino in the Hotel Nacional de Cuba, the beautiful Havana hotel opened in 1930 that had been designed by McKim, Mead and White the leading architectural firm of the time. The firm also designed some of New York City's monumental buildings, including the original Pennsylvania Station, the Metropolitan Museum of Art, the Villard Houses, Strivers' Row in Harlem, the Harvard Club and the original Madison Square Garden—which was an upscale residential building that housed a famous restaurant on its roof—as well as many other Beaux Arts–influenced projects. In reality, Marden, who was well known for his outgoing and agreeable personality, was the public face for the people who really controlled the Hotel Nacional: Meyer Lansky and his brother, Jake. Ben Marden had come full circle from his days as the operator of the Colonial Inn.

In the United States Department of State Dispatch No. 1410, dated February 29 1952, Ben Marden was mentioned as having funded the acquisition of Radio Habana Cuba (RHC). The RHC Cadena Azul network had been purchased from Amado Trinidad for $1 million. The state department dispatch noted that the leader of the group "is reliably stated to be Ben Marden former owner of the Riviera nightclub outside New York City." The communiqué reported that Edmund A. Chester, former vice-president of the Columbia Broadcasting System (CBS), was the new president and that Clarence Alexander of the Dumont Television Network had been appointed the new manager of Radio Habana Cuba. In addition, the group had planned to start bringing in TV service to the six Cuban provinces: Habana, Matanzas, Santa Clara, Ciego de Avila, Camaguey and Santiago. Marden was again a friendly face representing Lansky and American interests that went as high as the White House. One of Marden's partners in the Habana radio deal was Elliot Roosevelt, son of President Franklin D. Roosevelt.

Marden left the nightclub business in 1946 and, for ten years, owned and operated the Playhouse Theater in New York, as well as financed several stage plays. It seems that he was able to sever his contacts with Lansky and the rest of his partners without diminishing his fortune or his health. Marden lived in Manhattan and Florida, where he was involved with charitable pursuits. He was a founder of the Albert Einstein College of Medicine of Yeshiva University, a favorite cause of wealthy Jewish New Yorkers in the 1950s. He also supported schools for children with special needs. Marden died at age seventy-seven in New York. Some years before, the doorman at the apartment building Marden owned had left Ben his entire estate of $30,000, noting in his will that "you are a kind man and you will know better how to utilize these monies for the good of people than anyone I know of."

BUILDING THE RIVIERA

One can imagine Ben Marden and his architect, Louis Allen Abramson, standing in the knee-deep snow during the harsh 1935–36 winter, checking on the progress of the construction crews as they struggled to break through the solid rock of the Palisades to form the foundation for Ben's new Riviera. Abramson was an outstanding and highly regarded architect whose thirty-four years of experience and list of notable designs included Longchamps Restaurants, Beth Israel Hospital, Zion Hospital and branches of the New York Public Library. Abramson at the time was also planning extensive renovations for New York's Belleview Hospital, which was built during the Civil War. They huddled together in their fedora hats and heavy overcoats and scrutinized the site plans, comparing them to the excavation they were witnessing.

After the dust had settled from days of dynamite blasting, the huge steel mesh blasting mats were removed to reveal a jagged crater estimated to be 13 feet deep, about 200 feet in length and 150 feet in width that was blasted out of the solid rock of the great natural wonder, the New Jersey Palisades. The excavated pit was then prepared for the pouring of the reinforced concrete walls for the new structure. The construction process would have been much easier if Ben Marden and his architect had agreed to use a slab-on-grade method of construction, but obviously Ben Marden wanted a huge basement in his new Riviera, and no manner of solid rock was going to stop him from having it. When the foundation pit was firmly set within its confines at the edge of the cliffs, wooden false work was constructed to accept the poured concrete that would form the basement walls. Certainly favors owed to Ben's partners by

The Riviera's Art Deco main entrance. *Courtesy of the Fort Lee Historical Society.*

contractors during the construction of the George Washington Bridge were most likely called in, thus ensuring the project's timely completion and union cooperation throughout the construction process.

The Riviera's basement was huge and housed five heavily designed concrete pads to act as the base for five oversized walk-in freezer boxes that allowed Ben's chefs to purchase high-quality provisions in quantity. Next, reinforced concrete piers were formed and poured to support intricate electromechanical devices with complex gears and hydraulics that were necessary to make the bandstand and stage revolve silently on the floor above.

The architectural plans called for the massive kitchen area to be located in the basement. In addition, the plans also showed a barbershop, a massage parlor, a tailor shop and a wine cellar to be similarly located in the basement. A straight concrete walkway ramp was then constructed leading upward, out of the basement and along the southernmost outside of the building toward the parking lot, spanning a distance of about seventy-five feet. This was used for the daily food and beverage deliveries. Jerry Bakounis, a beverage delivery man from Fort Lee, used this entrance regularly for sometimes two

The Riviera's waiters preparing to cater to patrons' every need. *Courtesy of the Fort Lee Historical Society.*

or three deliveries a day of soft drinks, Saratoga bottled water, mixers and special brands of beverages ordered by the headliners.

The interior basement stairs leading to the dining room were about nine feet in width, with a stainless steel and brass handrail running down the middle that prevented the waiters going in and out of the dining room from bumping into one another as they delicately balanced huge round aluminum trays overhead. At the top of the stairs were double swinging doors leading to the dining room.

The main level of the building was something to behold. It must have been the architect's plan to give the Art Deco building nautical characteristics, a look attributable to the fact that it overlooked the river. Almost everyone who remembers the Riviera would probably agree that it resembled the bridge of an ocean liner, especially since it was strategically located at the very edge of the Palisades. The building was constructed of masonry, with a flat roof. Unlike the old Riviera's wooden structure, Marden built his new dream to last. All exterior walls were made of reinforced block and concrete, with a finish parget of smooth stucco with soft, rounded surfaces.

The grand Art Deco main entrance to the Riviera was in the rear of the building because the front sat at the cliff's edge. A series of five steps sweeping in a gentle curve welcomed the parties of people as they exited their cars and limousines. After the uniformed doorman opened the car doors and greeted the guests, carhops—usually a roster of ten, mostly young local men from Fort Lee—would drive the vehicles away and park them in the main parking lot or across Hudson Terrace in the auxiliary parking lot—or even up and down Hudson Terrace, as when Tony Martin and Frank Sinatra appeared. Another elegantly attired doorman stood at the top of the exterior steps and welcomed guests as he held open the large brass doors.

Upon entering the building, patrons would drift to the left side of the vast club and pass through the Serpentine Bar and lounge area, where paintings were displayed over the lounge couches. Although Ashile Gorky was credited with the artwork in the Riviera, another noted artist, Saul Schary, produced all of the framed oils and watercolors and wall murals. Gorky and Schary painted in a similar abstract impressionist style, but Gorky was one of the most

The Riviera's lounge, adorned by contemporary art especially commissioned by Ben Marden. *Courtesy of the Fort Lee Historical Society.*

influential artists of his time. Gorky had painted the large pieces that hung in the original Riviera and that were destroyed in the building's fire. Marden asked Gorky, whose work was very popular in the 1940s, to paint murals on the Riviera's cocktail lounge walls. He did some drawings for Marden, which would be priceless today, but they were lost. After years of critical success, and years of misfortune, Gorky took his own life in 1948 at the age of forty-four.

The thick carpeting throughout the building featured Ben Marden's initials woven into the fabric. That was an enormous statement about Ben's ego and his desire to let the world know who he was and that he had constructed an iconic showplace. As the patrons continued their walk through the lounge area, they passed the hatcheck room and the souvenir concession stand, where photos were available to be picked up at the end of the evening. Oh yes, there were also photo girls, cigarette girls and hatcheck girls. You name it, and they were there, all glamorous and smiling. No detail of opulence and service was left to chance.

The man who ran the concessions at the Riviera was Al Quain. He also ran the parking lot, which was a constant source of problems for the Riviera's management. Occasionally, the carhops would take joy rides around the towns in beautiful new Cadillacs and even Dusenbergs to show off the cars to their friends. Many parties leaving the Riviera late in the evening or early in the morning found that their cars were difficult to immediately locate. Pupi Campo, the personable Latin orchestra leader who customarily would stand outside the stage door during his breaks to take in some fresh air, would console the concerned car owner by saying, "Wha hoppen, baby?" and kidding with them until their vehicle was located, most typically within the hour. Campo was married to Betty Clooney, sister of Rosemary Clooney, and he is actor George Clooney's uncle. Needless to say, there was great turnover in the Riviera's parking attendants, as they were usually fired as soon as they returned the customer's car.

One story, confirmed by the Fort Lee Police Department, told of a few of the local boys who, while walking along Hudson Terrace during a summer night in 1952, decided to take a couple of Cadillacs for a joy ride. The keys to the cars were typically left under the floor mats by the Riviera's carhops, so stealing a car was an easy thing to do. After driving around for a while, the boys thought that it would be a good idea to drive the cars up to a place in Englewood Cliffs called the "Quarry" (because it actually had been one years before). The boys then pushed the cars off the side of the quarry, completely destroying the Cadillacs. The boys were quickly apprehended by Englewood and Fort Lee police because so many of their friends had seen

The Riviera hatcheck girls. *Courtesy of the Fort Lee Historical Society.*

them driving the stolen cars. They were spared from jail sentences, but their parents had to pay for the purchase of two new Cadillacs.

We return to the floor plan of the club. As patrons passed the hatcheck and entered a wide, low ceiling corridor about twenty-five feet long, they could opt to turn left and walk down another corridor that was dimly lit. Although nondescript, this corridor led to the most notorious and infamous part of the club. It was here where knowledgeable people could gain entrance to the Riviera's dazzling and illegal gambling casino. Patrons would slip past the men's and ladies' rooms unnoticed and then enter a janitor's closet on the left of the hallway, closing the door behind them. They would find themselves in a typical dimly lit janitor's closet, complete with slop sink, random scrub buckets, mops and brooms. Over in the corner of the closet was a pedestal floor fan, similar to the many fans found in the dining room. It was obviously stored there because it was presumed that the fan did not work. The fan's electric plug hung from the fan's cage. When one took the electric cord from that innocent-looking fan and plugged it into the nearby wall socket, the adjacent wall would slide

The three-tiered dining room at the Riviera. *Courtesy of the Fort Lee Historical Society.*

away completely, revealing an elegant, eight-foot-wide, gently winding staircase complete with clear glass handrails on both sides leading up to a hidden level of the building. Again the plush red carpet was emblazoned with the initials "BM." It's truly fascinating to think about who among the rich and famous (and infamous) stood in that janitor's closet and plugged the fan cord into the wall to gain access to Ben Marden's fabled casino.

The casino's walls at the top of the stairs were covered with large leather mauve-colored squares. The dimensions of the room were about fifty by sixty-five feet. In addition, there was a room called, by those in the know, the "machine gun room." In actuality, there were no machine guns in that room, but there was a peephole that afforded a view of the entire showroom below. The peephole was carefully placed to stage left by the mural on the side of the entrance to the showroom. The peephole was constantly manned, to keep tabs on the law enforcement people, powerful politicians, judges and even rival mobsters who entered the club.

Back down stairs on the main level, patrons would exit the janitor's closet after trying their luck at craps, blackjack, roulette or other illegal games

A spectacular view from the Riviera's dining room, which overlooked the George Washington Bridge. *Courtesy of the Fort Lee Historical Society.*

of chance. As they entered the showroom on their left, they were greeted by the maitre d' and waiter captains. Frank Bruno, Joe Bonardio and Lou Gallo, the waiter captains, would flick their wrists with two fingers in the air, indicating that this party needed to be seated. If a substantial gratuity was inconspicuously placed in the palm of the captain via a friendly handshake, the couple might very well be favored with a ringside table.

Always on hand in the dining room were the photo girls, who would take pictures of couples and groups with Speed Graphic press cameras and then sell the souvenir photos to them for $1.50 in a Riviera folder, which would be available at the end of the evening fresh from the Riviera's photography lab. There were also cigarette girls, who would roam throughout the audience dressed in their French maid attire and carry a flat box with low sides filled with all different brands of cigarettes: Pall Mall, Old Gold, Chesterfields, Camels—any kind and they had them. The fourteen- by twelve-inch rectangular tray was carried waist high across their midriff and was fastened by a ribbon that went around their necks, thus freeing their hands to dispense the cigarettes and collect the money. Friendly and flirtatious smiles went a long way in encouraging nice tips.

The famous round roof that opened up to the sky. *Courtesy of the Fort Lee Historical Society.*

The Riviera's stage door to the right of the main entrance. *Courtesy of the Fort Lee Historical Society.*

The Donn Arden showgirls posing in front of the mauve leather wall in the Riviera's gambling casino. *Courtesy of the Austin family collection.*

The Riviera even had a house physician. Marden, and later Miller, employed doctors who spent part of every day at the nightclub, seeing staff members who had submitted workman's compensation claims, chorus girls and musicians who needed the attention of a doctor and patrons in need of emergency services. The house physician from 1951 to the Riviera's closing in 1953 was Arthur Shapiro. Dr. Shapiro had recently graduated from medical school and was finishing his internship when his cousin, a waiter captain at the club, suggested that he apply for the open position of house doctor. Dr. Shapiro spent two happy years at the Riviera taking care of the staff, watching rehearsals and meeting the stars. He lives in Las Vegas and was interviewed in 2011. Dr. Shapiro's cousin was Joe Marsh, who after his time as a waiter captain at the Riviera went on to operate the popular Spindle Top restaurant in Manhattan. His partner in that enterprise was Meyer Lansky's son-in-law.

An ample supply of black Bakelite ashtrays with the Riviera's name on them was always on hand. The customers could easily slip them into their purse or pocket, which was expected by Abe Vine, the Riviera's purchasing agent. Even the ever changing menus were designed to be carried out of the building, which were great for advertising the Riviera.

There were three choices for seating, and the cover charge was $3.50 per person. This charge was added to bar and restaurant checks as a way to recover the cost of the elaborate stage shows. After entering the showroom, patrons led by a waiter captain would step down three steps onto the lowest part of the room. At this level, ringside tables were available. To the left were four steps leading to the window seats on the terraced level that wrapped around the showroom in a horseshoe shape. These tables took in the excellent views of the George Washington Bridge and the New York skyline. Below it, but still above the lowest ringside level, was another terraced level that was about stage high. Ringside tables looked up at the stage. The first terraced level was eye level with the stage, and the horseshoe-shaped upper level looked slightly down at the stage, which meant that patrons had great views of the stage no matter where they sat.

The stage or dance floor was rectangular in shape, except for the end, which jutted out into the audience and was shaped like an oval. The dance floor had a revolving center section about twenty feet in diameter with a fifteen-foot radius that was turned by electricity. The dance floor had an elevation of about four feet above the ringside tables. The tiered revolving bandstand was round, with the circle divided in half and separated by a soundproof wall. The reason for the separation was to allow two orchestras to be seated and ready to perform. When one orchestra would finish playing, the bandstand would revolve, revealing the other orchestra. The music would never actually stop, and the audience would hear the music from one orchestra fade as the bandstand revolved, introducing the music of the next orchestra.

The center section of the tiered ceiling above the showroom was shaped like a round cake and could rise up and roll off to the side. In that section

A chip from the Riviera's casino depicting the George Washington Bridge. *Courtesy of the Fort Lee Historical Society.*

The new Ben Marden's Riviera. *Courtesy of the Fort Lee Historical Society.*

of the ceiling, just below the removable roof, was the spotlight booth. This is where two electricians or spotlight men would work the lamps. The huge windows surrounding the river side of the building slid down into the floor like power windows on an automobile. Since the building was built in 1936, central air conditioning was not available, and floor fans mounted on pedestals were used throughout the club during the summer and provided a degree of comfort. The menu featured the finest steaks and chops; however, things as simple as club sandwiches, hamburgers and Chinese dishes were also available. Some people did not come to the Riviera to have dinner but instead came to see the show and have cocktails. Attendants were everywhere; patrons couldn't put a cigarette into their mouths without a well-groomed attendant reaching over with a Ronson lighter and lighting it for them. The guests left with the feeling that they were special, and that was the trademark Ben Marden touch.

Returning to the exterior of the building, one could not help but be impressed with the unusual Art Deco design and visual appeal. The building looked like a great ship waiting to be launched into the Hudson River from the top of the Palisades, hundreds of feet above the water. The design was nautical, with the round porthole windows spaced evenly around the

A magazine spread from the 1940s covering Ben Marden's Riviera. *Courtesy of the Fort Lee Historical Society.*

building. The exterior paint colors used on the building were bright blue and bright yellow. These colors on their own might be considered hideous, but when applied to support the building's nautical look, they were absolutely perfect and unforgettable. Coincidently, the colors on the exterior of the Riviera were likened to carnival-type colors used at Palisades Amusement Park and even at Luna Park at Coney Island. Like on a ship, brass was everywhere; from the grand main entrance to the handrails throughout the building, brass was the metal of choice. The stage was even ringed in shiny brass. Marden, and later Bill Miller, had crews on hand just to attend to the brass in and around the club. The Art Deco nautical theme prevailed throughout the building.

The men's room and the ladies' room had ever present attendants. Fresh towels, hair tonic, cologne, combs, brushes, mouthwash and feminine products were always at the ready if needed. There was a shoeshine attendant on duty in the men's room to spruce up a tarnished pair of shoes. The Riviera tried to anticipate everyone's needs so that the experience of dining and dancing, along with seeing the top performers in show business, would be an unforgettable experience.

The building itself served as its own advertisement, if you consider that every person coming across the George Washington Bridge had no choice but to look at the fabulous Abramson architectural design decked out in bright blue and yellow colors. It was topped off by a gigantic, highly illuminated sign on the roof spanning sixty-five feet across, with letters eight feet high, sporting either Ben Marden's or Bill Miller's Riviera and lighting the sky over the Hudson. The free advertising it generated was priceless to a nightclub that was really America's Showplace.

After entering the stage door, which was located to the right of the main entrance, the performers would ascend four steps to the bandstand level. At the top of these steps was a door on the right with a star on it, and that was the featured headliner's dressing room. This was the dressing room that Tony Martin, Sinatra, Vic Damone, Sammy Davis Jr., Joey Bishop and many other stars would use when they were playing the Riviera. If visitors turned to the left of the dressing room, they would find themselves behind the side of the bandstand not in use at the moment. Another left would lead to the chorus girls' dressing room. Mary Smith, the wardrobe mistress, would always be busy mending costumes and making adjustments. Mary, an older Irish woman, acted as a surrogate mother to the girls and gave them sage advice, as well as a piece of her mind if they got out of line, as they often did.

Mrs. O'Rourke lived in the Coytesville section of Fort Lee about a block away from the old Villa Richard, on Eighth Street. Her husband was the day security officer at the Riviera, and she would prepare the stage makeup for the girls. She would also solicit anyone she could find to agree to make false eyelashes for the showgirls. Making eyelashes was almost an impossible task. She would supply an envelope with Asian hair, a thing that looked like a very thin pipe cleaner and a pair of tweezers. The person making the eyelash would then have to tie the hair around the pipe cleaner with the tweezers. Mrs. O'Rourke would pay sixty cents each for false eyelashes.

Leaving wardrobe, if one took the metal stairs, they would go to the second floor, where the additional stars' dressing rooms were located. One night, Jimmy Durante, who was using the second-floor dressing room, was having a major craps game with five others on a blanket in his dressing room. When Al Austin, the security guard, got word that the chief of the Fort Lee Police Department, Fred Stengel, was about to visit the club with the mayor, he went up to Durante's dressing room and told them to stop shooting craps because the mayor was dropping by for a visit. Durante, in his own inimitable way, then said, "Stop the music—I mean stop the game, we're being raided," and burst out laughing. He then picked up all the money on the blanket and began stuffing it into Austin's police uniform and said that "if anyone's going to be arrested, it's going to be you." Later that evening, Austin returned the money to Durante.

Ben Marden's dream became a reality. The Riviera was bigger than life, and it was the destination for the most elegant people in New York's night scene. The time was the zenith of the nightclub era, and the Riviera stood alone as the greatest nightclub in the nation.

1946

THE YEAR BILL MILLER
BOUGHT THE RIVIERA

B ill Miller negotiating to buy out Ben Marden's shares of the Riviera and reopening it were not the only exciting things happening in 1946. For the first time, the U.S. Army bounced radar signals off the lunar surface from Belmar, New Jersey. In addition to that, a press conference was held at the University of Pennsylvania announcing a new invention called an Electronic Numerical Integrator and Calculator (ENIAC). The new device was the first computer.

The machine took up an entire room, weighed thirty tons and came to life using more than eighteen thousand vacuum tubes to perform its functions, such as counting to five thousand in a single second. The computer cost $450,000 to build and was designed by the army to calculate artillery trajectories.

It was in that same year that the UN established the International Atomic Energy Commission—could it be because a patent was filed with the United States Patent Office for the H-bomb on May 26? It's no wonder that the U.S. government built its first rocket to leave earth's atmosphere that year. The rocket reached a height of fifty miles. Not too bad for a first try.

With all of that atomic activity going on, it was feared that foreign powers, such as the USSR and China, might be trying to steal our secrets, so President Truman set up the Central Intelligence Group (CIG), an outgrowth of the Office of Strategic Services (OSS), directed by Colonel "Wild" Bill Donovan, a former Wall Street lawyer turned spy. Late in 1945, Truman coordinated various intelligence reform plans and created the CIG. It was not until 1947 that it was renamed the Central Intelligence Agency.

Winston Churchill, speaking as the guest of President Truman at Westminster College in Fulton, Missouri, delivered his "Sinews of Peace" speech, later known as the "Iron Curtain" speech, in which the term became a part of general language usage for decades.

As New York City began to become more and more congested, and getting from one place to the other became increasingly more frustrating, the first commercial helicopter license was issued in the city. The United Nations also set up its temporary headquarters at Hunter College, moving from San Francisco. The UN then moved to Lake Success, New York, on Long Island, where it stayed until its headquarters was built along Manhattan's East River on land contributed by the Rockefeller family.

Ho Chi Minh was elected president of the Democratic Republic of Vietnam in March of that year, the League of Nations held its last session in Geneva and Weight Watchers was formed.

The year 1946 was one of awakening for the nation. Soldiers, sailors and marines were returning home from overseas, and the first thing on their minds was to get married or, if they were already married, find an affordable home to live in and pick up where they left off before the war. However, before they could start looking for that home, they first had to find a job. Many veterans found work at the Ford Motor Company in nearby Edgewater, New Jersey, only about two miles from Fort Lee. The Ford Motor Company was in the process of switching over to civilian vehicles once again from its wartime assembly line schedule of pushing out military cars and trucks. Locals would tell you that just about every guy working on the assembly line would play the illegal "numbers" game on a daily basis. Unlike upstairs at the Riviera and the big bets placed there, the numbers were on a smaller scale, designed for the working guy, and they seemed to satisfy everyone's need to risk a few dollars in hopes of getting a big payoff.

The average cost of a newly built home in 1946 was $5,600.00, and the average-priced resale home was just about $1,500.00. Gasoline could be bought for $0.15 per gallon. Although prices sound cheap back then, one must consider that the average wage per year was only $2,500.00.

Although things seemed to be going fine in our country, in China 30 million people were close to dying from starvation. In the United States, however, sugar and most food supplies unavailable during the war were rapidly returning to the neighborhood grocery stores.

In 1946, the U.S. government began atomic bomb testing on Bikini Atoll in the Pacific Ocean, and Paris fashion news was not far behind in advertising a new type of women's swimsuit that took the world by storm. It was called the "bikini." When the first Cannes film festival took place that year, the beaches of Cannes were filled with filmdom's lovelies sporting their new bikinis.

Although things seemed to be going great for some in the world, many people were still suffering from the ravages of World War II. From June through September of that year, 100,000 Jews left Poland and traveled through Czechoslovakia to displaced persons camps in Germany. People carried smiles on the outside and great sadness on the inside. The war had taken its toll on all sides, with America suffering the loss of many of its sons and daughters in the military. An unofficial estimate indicates that 408,000 servicemen and woman were killed and about 671,000 were wounded in the conflict.

Coinciding with the end of the war, the Japanese internment camps established in the United States under the 1942 U.S. Executive Order No. 9066 were closed for good. The camps, which were clearly unconstitutional and illegal on every level, were the brainchild of then California attorney general Earl Warren, who was later appointed chief justice of the United States Supreme Court by President Eisenhower. The Warren Court distinguished itself with important rulings that established civil rights for all Americans. Warren and the court's majority wrote brilliant opinions protecting individual rights that became the law of the land. While his work on the court was exemplarily, he later lost credibility when the Warren Commission investigated the assassination of John F. Kennedy and drew conclusions that were erroneous.

Still, the world must go on, as our instincts for survival mandate. Following that premise, those who survived picked up where they left off and continued on. As life continued and families got back together, war babies resulted. Susan Sarandon, Tommy Lee Jones, Candice Bergen, Tyne Daly, Uri Geller, Dolly Parton, Donald Trump, Steven Spielberg, Sly Stallone, Cher, George Walker Bush Jr. and Bill Clinton were all welcomed into the world in 1946. On July 14, 1946, Dr. Benjamin Spock published his book called *The Common Sense Book of Baby and Child Care*, the definitive book on raising children at that time.

Following a wartime Democratic presidential administration, the Republicans took control of the Senate and House in midterm elections. Also that year, John F. Kennedy (D-Mass) was elected to the House of Representatives.

Sports played an important part as recreational outlets for so many Americans at that time in history. One of the most popular sporting events that year was the second Joe Louis v. Billy Conn fight. The first fight had been held at the Polo Grounds on June 18, 1941. On that date, the fight was billed as "David v. Goliath." Conn was probably the best small heavyweight who ever boxed. He could do it all: he blocked punches, had a terrific left hand, was quick and agile on his feet and was technically almost perfect in every way. He could even take a terrific punch and quickly recuperate from it.

On that particular night back in 1941, Conn won almost every round fighting against the huge and powerful Joe Louis. For twelve rounds, Conn was ahead on the judge's cards. In the twelfth round, Conn staggered Louis with a powerful left hook that stunned Louis. He did not go down, however, and was saved by the bell. All Conn had to do was avoid Louis for the next three rounds, and he would have won the fight and taken the title as heavyweight champion of the world. Conn, on the other hand, had his own ego at stake and tried valiantly to knock out the Brown Bomber. That was when he made his mistake. Louis released a volley of lefts and rights to the head that sent Conn reeling. With a final right hand to Conn's head, Conn went down, unable to recover and was counted out. When asked so many times why he did not stay away from Louis during the last three rounds, Conn exclaimed, "What's the use of being Irish if you can't be thick?"

The first televised title boxing match took place in 1946 in New York as Joe Louis again took on Billy Conn. Three NBC stations carried the fight that night. You can bet that the room upstairs at the Riviera was humming that night. Maybe you guessed it: Louis won that one, too.

The entertainment world was going strong in 1946. Frank Sinatra had a major hit on his hands with "Day by Day," and Frankie Lane also topped the charts with his hit "That's My Desire."

The Flamingo Casino opened that year in Las Vegas. It was Buddy Wilkerson who designed the casino and then sold a controlling interest to Bugsy Siegel. In fact, the Flamingo happened to be the third hotel on the Las Vegas Strip. At that time, it was not even considered that Las Vegas would be any competition to the Riviera or anything that was going on in Cuba.

Siegel and his business partners must have had some inclination that Cuba might have some issues that could eventually be bad for business after the war, and maybe that's why they decided to invest so heavily in Las Vegas. It is amazing to think that although books, films and television programs portray them as just mobsters, in reality they were brilliant businesspeople.

In 1946, Cuba and its legal gambling casinos were very busy hosting Americans, especially during the winter months. Visitors to Cuba from the East Coast took the Florida East Coast Railway's Havana Special from New

York's Pennsylvania Station to Miami and then switched to a local train to the Florida Keys. An overnight steamer brought them to Havana. Pan American World Airways' first regular overseas Clipper flight was to Havana from New York.

Chemist H.B. Parmele filed an internal report at Lorillard Tobacco Company that noted, "Certain scientists and medical authorities have claimed for many years that the use of tobacco contributes to cancer development in susceptible people. Just enough evidence has been presented to justify the possibility of such a presumption."

In 1946, Dean Martin and Jerry Lewis made their debuts at Skinny Damato's 500 Club in Atlantic City. They had worked hard at developing their act and had a very scripted routine. During their first show of the evening at the club, their act bombed. Dean and Jerry went backstage and decided to forget the script and just play to each other instead of playing to the audience. Jerry decided to just act crazy and run around on the stage, trying to bother Dean while he was singing. For the second show, Jerry came out wearing a busboys outfit and started dropping plates and annoying Dean. The audience went into hysterics watching the two cavort on stage, chasing each other around and throwing things. That was all that was needed to break up the house. They would do whatever popped into their heads. Their success at the 500 Club led to a string of appearances on the East Coast, ending with appearances and rave reviews at both Bill Miller's Riviera and the Copacabana.

With the end of World War II, people began to settle down and allow themselves the luxury of developing their hopes and dreams. Fort Lee began changing, too. For example, the A&P store in the Coytesville section of Fort Lee—a very small store with four employees who tallied up grocery bills with crayons, by hand, on the side of a brown paper bag—was replaced by a giant new store called Food Fair over in the Linwood Park section.

The Linwood Ball Field on Linwood Avenue, the field whose home team was the Coytesville AC's, was replaced by the Linwood Apartments. The apartments were the first buildings to be built in Fort Lee since before the war. There were a lot of show business people living in these buildings when they were first built. For example, there was Dolly Dawn, the lead singer of the Dawn Patrol; Phil Foster; Joey Bishop; and quite a few others who were in some way or another connected with show business.

Bill Miller was also about to realize his ultimate dream of owning the Riviera. The Riviera had been closed during the war, like so many other nightclubs of the time, mainly due to the lack of patronage caused by so many men and women being pressed into military service, short supplies of food and whiskey and the lack of gasoline to fuel the automobiles necessary to transport people.

Ben Marden had other, more pressing issues at hand, and selling the Riviera at this time seemed to be the right thing to do. Maybe Ben being fully aware that there was another place on the horizon called Las Vegas that was beginning to show promise gave impetus to his decision to sell the club. His Cuban interests also probably played a major part in his decision to sell. It's possible that Ben had some insight as to what was in store for Cuba in the coming years, and selling out at this time might have been the best move he could have made under the circumstances. Nevertheless, he had a ready buyer who was willing to put money on the table to take over the Riviera, and that buyer was Bill Miller. At this juncture, Miller was a seasoned professional entrepreneur full of energy, with a zest for taking risks.

BILL MILLER AND THE RIVIERA YEARS

B ill Miller was born in 1904 in Pinsk, Russia. His mother, Lena, and father, David, of the Jewish faith immigrated to the United States when he was one year old. Miller believed that his true Russian name had been lost at Ellis Island when government inspectors who couldn't spell the complicated eastern European names uttered by the immigrants would write down an easy or Anglicized version on the tags tied to a traveler's buttonhole.

Upon arriving in the United States, Bill's family settled in Brooklyn, New York, in a teeming slum along with thousands of other Jewish and Italian immigrants, all seeking the American dream. His father was a talented carpenter and builder, and soon the family moved to a better apartment in a brownstone-type building with only eight other families that boasted indoor plumbing and a window in each room. Because of his ability to work with tools, David Miller always managed to find better-paying jobs, and eventually the Millers moved to a new apartment building in Jersey City, New Jersey. The members of the Miller family were reasonably well provided for and lived comfortably, even though almost everyone else in their neighborhood was trying to survive on the low wages and unsafe working conditions they were forced to accept as immigrant families in a new country.

Bill Miller studied the violin beginning on his tenth birthday. His father would routinely give him fifty cents per week to pay for lessons. One day, while playing hooky from school, Miller spent his fifty cents for a ticket to see his first vaudeville show with a few of his neighborhood chums. He was so impressed with the fast-paced, multiple stage acts—including singers, magicians, comics, dog acts and especially the dancers found in every vaudeville show—that he realized that he wanted to become part of show business. Years later, Miller said he was actually mesmerized by the way dancers executed intricate routines. On successive visits to the vaudeville shows, Miller would memorize the pattern of the dancers' steps, and in time their moves became indelibly imprinted in his mind. He practiced steps when he was alone at home and managed to perfect his own dance routine without ever taking a lesson.

In 1920, Bill auditioned for an amateur talent show held in a local movie theater. It was there where he met another young dancer named Nat Peterson who, like Bill, had a wild desire to try his luck in show business. Together they teamed up and developed a dance routine. Their next step was to search for a talent agent who could find them some engagements. After locating that agent, and with the young Miller pitching their talents with gusto, the agent was sold on the boys' potential of what they had to offer rather than what they actually had to offer. The agent was so impressed with young Miller that he presented Miller and Peterson with a contract on the spot. The two young hoofers had landed their first job in show business, and at the famous Palace Theater Ballroom on Broadway no less, with a salary of seventy-five dollars per week, an impressive wage for two young dancers taking on their first job.

Frank Sinatra with Riviera barber Rocky Vitetta. *Courtesy of the Rocky Vitetta collection.*

Nothing could stop Miller as he embarked on his new show business career. He quickly put together his own dance revue and kept the dancers working steadily for almost twelve years. At some point in time, it became obvious to him that after the years of dancing and nearing the age of thirty, the physical strain was taking its toll, and not just on his legs—he wasn't earning enough to support the upscale lifestyle to which he had become accustomed. It was a life-changing decision for Bill when he decided to hang up his tap shoes and give up dancing entirely, something he loved and something that had become the central part of his life. He did consider opening a dance academy and teaching the young performers who were filling the ranks of dancers for the great Broadway revues and the new nightclubs that were springing up in New York. But Miller knew that teaching dance still wouldn't be enough for him. He needed to be out there, taking chances, but definitely not as a performer.

Miller came to the realization that talent agents were involved with every aspect of show business. It was an easy transition. He had so many contacts that he had developed over twelve years in show business due to his likable manner. Miller then segued to become a Manhattan talent agent, sharing small offices in both the fabled Brill Building and at 1650 Broadway, the behind-the-scenes centers of show business in New York. Miller put together his own collection of acts for booking into national theater chains, nightclubs and resort hotels. It was far more profitable to be an agent and much easier than having to constantly rehearse and stay in top shape.

Spending twelve years in show business served as an excellent apprenticeship period, and Miller quickly became a successful talent agent. His little black book of phone numbers collected over his years as a dancer, in conjunction with enjoying a reputation as being a dependable man of his word, ensured that he was able to establish ongoing business relationships with the most important nightclub owners. Like a coach on a baseball team, Miller had the ability of getting the most out of his acts in order to position them so that they made the most favorable impressions during auditions. He would devise ways to present talent to audiences in a manner that had not been seen before. In addition, he always knew what acts to present to specific audiences. Miller's fame spread within the show business community, and his financial position improved considerably.

As a talent agent, Miller was always looking for new venues for his clients. Everyone in the business knew about show business legend Ben Marden and his ventures. After Ben acquired the Villa Richard, Miller would drive to New Jersey and visit what was now the Riviera to pitch his clients to Marden. Miller's likable personality and excellent insights as to what audiences liked earned him Marden's respect. Marden was very pleased to engage the services of someone who was so focused on booking the show talent for the legitimate end of Marden's business, leaving Marden free to handle the "other" end of the business. Miller, on the other hand, was equally pleased and impressed with Marden. He considered Marden a classy guy who controlled the greatest nightclub in the country—someone Miller could pattern himself after, a guy just like himself, but with lots of money and power. In fact, Marden was just what Miller fancied himself to be, and perhaps Marden saw something in Miller that reminded him of his own young days. There was only one important difference between them: Miller wasn't comfortable with the illegal gambling casino hidden on the Riviera's top floor or with Marden's seemingly close ties to the underworld. As a realist, though, Miller understood what the relationship with the mobsters could provide, but he wasn't enthusiastic about becoming connected to it. However, Miller's own career, beginning in New York and moving to Las Vegas in the 1950s, always shadowed the top figures in America's crime families.

Miller never missed an opportunity, and that opportunity came when he took on the job of managing Luna Park at the famed Coney Island. When World War II started, the Danzigers, managing partners of Luna Park, began to lose their top personnel to the military. Bill Miller, being at the right place at the right time, managed to work himself into a partnership in the business. Still, Bill knew that the real excitement and money he yearned for was not in being an agent for talent or owning a piece of Luna Park but instead being the boss and owning a first-class nightclub or major hotel.

Some time after meeting Marden and studying his business moves like he had done in his early days watching dancers, Miller was convinced that the time was right and that he, too, should strike out on his own and operate a nightclub. The Embassy, a club that was available on Manhattan's not-yet-fashionable East Side, was ready for new management. Located in a less than desirable section of the city made the club seem a bit dangerous and attractive to successful and wealthy patrons, and this is where Bill gained experience and learned the nightclub business.

Miller and his new Embassy Club got off to a terrific start, with lavish floor shows in which Miller showcased his own acts, but no matter how hard Miller tried, he couldn't keep up the momentum of packing the house on a nightly basis, and soon the Embassy's neon luster began to fade. Miller was almost broke at this point, having financed the Embassy Club himself,

A partial view of the new Riviera on the Palisades. *Courtesy of the Fort Lee Historical Society.*

The new Showplace of America, high on the cliffs. *Courtesy of the Fort Lee Historical Society.*

THE
RIVIERA
OF
AMERICA

JUST ACROSS
THE GEORGE
WASHINGTON
BRIDGE

BEN MARDEN'S
RIVIERA

Above: The main
entrance of the new
Ben Marden's Riviera.
*Courtesy of the Fort Lee
Historical Society.*

Left and next page:
A coveted and
collectable menu from
the original Riviera.
*Courtesy of the Fort Lee
Historical Society.*

Menu

PREMIERE DINNER SIX DOLLARS   POPULAR PRICES THEREAFTER

Fresh Fruit Supreme Kummel and Maraschino

Hearts of Celery   Mixed Olives   Almonds

———

Soup Riviera

———

Filet of Sole Veronique

———

Stuffed Royal Squab Perigourdines

Filet Mignon Rossini with Fresh Mushrooms

New Boiled Potatoes—Parisienne with Parsley
New Peas a la Francaise

———

Salade Pierrote

———

Baba au Rhum

Assorted Mints   Moka

Above left: Ben Marden's Riviera matchbook (original). *Courtesy of the Fort Lee Historical Society.*

Above right: Ben Marden's Riviera matchbook (new). *Courtesy of the Fort Lee Historical Society.*

Bill Miller's Riviera photo holder. *Courtesy of the Fort Lee Historical Society.*

A Riviera casino chip. *Courtesy of the Fort Lee Historical Society.*

The Riviera's nautical design. *Courtesy of the Fort Lee Historical Society.*

The Riviera's famous Serpentine Bar. *Courtesy of the Fort Lee Historical Society.*

A souvenir of Bill Miller's Riviera. *Courtesy of the Fort Lee Historical Society.*

The cover of Riviera's souvenir photo album. *Courtesy of the Fort Lee Historical Society.*

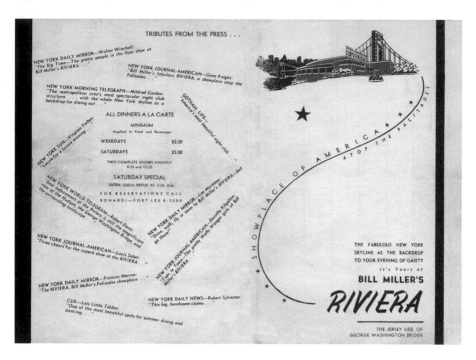

Rave notices from the press. *Courtesy of the Fort Lee Historical Society.*

Now it's Bill Miller's Riviera. *Courtesy of the Fort Lee Historical Society.*

Band leader Pupi
Campo and his
skimmer hat.
*Courtesy of the Austin
family collection.*

but his enthusiasm remained high, and when he decided to sell the club, he
never believed that it was he who had failed. Quite the contrary, he believed
that the club was not big enough for him and his dreams of booking major
stars and huge musical reviews along with name bands.

The purchaser Miller found to buy out his part of the Embassy was Sam
Marcus, who had other business interests and was intrigued with owning a
nightclub. Marcus was in the photographic supply business, centered in New
York City at the time. After taking over the Embassy, Marcus, like Miller,
enjoyed a great opening period, but once again the Embassy could not
sustain itself as a successful operation. Some said that it was because of city
ordinances that permitted dancing only in hotel ballrooms and prohibited
it in nightclubs. Eventually, Sam Marcus also realized that as much as he
loved being a club owner, it was time to get out. He sold the club to David
Loew of the Loews Theaters family in 1948. Loews Theaters was the parent
company of Metro-Goldwyn-Mayer (MGM).

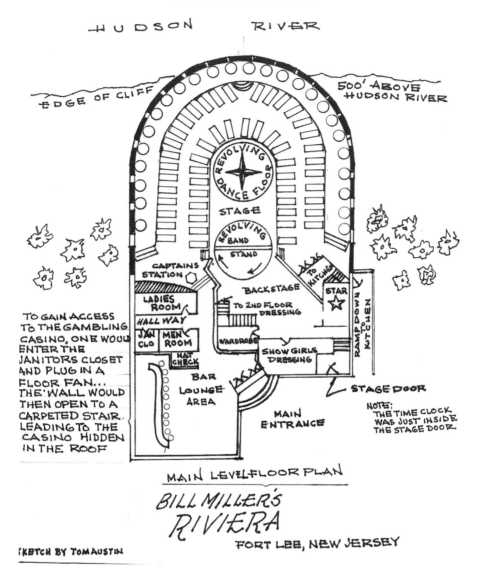

The Riviera's floor plan. *Courtesy of the Austin family collection.*

Miller's desire to own a big-time nightclub just got stronger. He started to evaluate the opportunities available for him. World War II was winding down, and there were many clubs that had closed due to the war, and they offered a number of opportunities. The one club that kept cropping up in Miller's mind, however, was that beautiful Riviera, situated on the New Jersey side of the Hudson River up on top of the cliffs overlooking the

George Washington Bridge. That was the trophy that Miller had his eye on. The only problem was that the Marden club was so involved with major mob figures, due to its notorious gambling casino, that to acquire it would take an enormous amount of money, which seemed to put the Riviera out of Miller's reach. Miller also knew that to buy the Riviera, one was also accepting the mob people who came along with the gambling, the liquor and even the table linens.

Miller, knowing that Sam Marcus had sold the Embassy and might be looking for another investment, approached Marcus and suggested that they throw in together and approach Ben Marden to find out if he would consider selling the Riviera to them. The idea must have worked because not only did Marden agree to sell the Riviera to Miller, but he was also willing to hold a purchase money mortgage for a period of a few years to allow Miller to get started and put his own brand on the Riviera. Soon the huge neon sign high over the Palisades was changed to "Bill Miller's Riviera."

The Riviera got off to a rocky start with Miller at the helm, mainly due to his lack of cash. However, Miller and Marcus did manage to acquire additional property close to the site for another parking lot from the Michael Realty Company. The price for the property was recorded as being only one dollar. When Miller took possession of the Riviera, he promised local officials that the gambling casino would remain closed. However, the hidden casino seemed to always be in use for "private parties," and what went on at those parties always remained a point of interest to the uninvited. However, gambling continued because it attracted wealthy patrons and the casino's profits helped pay the salaries of the top show business personalities appearing at the Riviera. The casino was kept out of the limelight, and whatever went on in that room upstairs always remained discreet.

As the months went by, Miller found himself deeper and deeper in financial trouble, and by the end of 1946, he was hovering on bankruptcy due to astronomical start-up costs. Deep in debt, he began making announcements to the press that he was contemplating opening up an amusement park next to the Riviera similar to the old Luna Park in Coney Island where Miller was involved years before. Along with the nightclub and amusement park, he even boasted of opening an exclusive swim club, complete with cabanas and poolside entertainment. As it turned out, all of the announcements were made just to stave off the creditors until the Riviera began to show a profit and Miller had the cash to pay the mounting bills associated with the operation of a first-class nightclub that employed more than one hundred people.

Tony Martin and his opening act at the Riviera, the Ritz Brothers. *Courtesy of the Austin family collection.*

Marden, a man of great patience, gave Miller time to succeed with the Riviera. That moment came when Miller first booked Tony Martin in to the club. Martin's shows were completely packed. A reservation for dinner and a show starring Tony Martin was the most sought-after ticket in New York. On some nights, the line of cars waiting to park at the Riviera stretched onto the George Washington Bridge, causing traffic jams. When Martin appeared in Fort Lee, the cars were parked from the George Washington Bridge plaza on Hudson Terrace all the way up north to the town of Englewood Cliffs. It seemed that everyone wanted to see and hear Tony Martin, the guy who made women swoon. The fact is that Tony Martin would bring so many people to the club that sometimes three shows a night were needed to fill the demand. Of course, Tony Martin didn't come cheap. Newspapers reported that Miller was paying out $10,000 per week just to pay Martin's salary.

Mobsters Frank Erickson and the Fischetti brothers from Chicago, as well as local gangsters Joe Adonis, Willie Moretti and Frank Costello, were frequent patrons of the Riviera, especially when the big acts like Frank Sinatra and Tony Martin appeared there. Politicians, mobsters and even clergymen flocked to the Riviera to see the lavish shows and enjoy the beautiful showgirls who danced and preened on the revolving stage. Once Miller gained a financial foothold and the Riviera became profitable, he paid off the existing purchase money mortgage held by Ben Marden and his financiers in 1947.

The famous Hallandale, Florida nightclub, the Colonial Inn, which Marden once owned, later became another target of Miller's wish list. As late as 1948, Bill tried to lease the main room, with the intention of putting Danny Thomas in there. His efforts went by the wayside when Hal Minsky, of the burlesque shows family, beat him to it and took over the club. Another New Yorker who operated the Colonial Inn for a while was Lew Walters, the famed owner of the glamorous Latin Quarter in New York City, which featured major stars. Lew's daughter, Barbara Walters, said in interviews, "Growing up surrounded by celebrities kept me from being in awe of them."

Like Marden, Miller was also said to have speculative financial interests in Cuba. As late as 1957, it was rumored among those who were interested

Tony Martin with Fort Lee fire chief Frank Schmidt, who responded to the fire that destroyed the original Riviera. *Courtesy of the Schmidt family collection.*

in offshore gambling that Miller had a large financial interest in a Havana hotel under construction called the Hotel Monte Carlo. The rumor further suggested Miller was slated to be its president and would operate the hotel as another Riviera, with the same high-class acts, lavish production and gambling, which was legal in Cuba. It's no wonder that back in the early 1950s, when the Riviera closed in October each year, practically every person working there moved to Cuba to work in hotels and casinos during the winter and returned in April when the Riviera reopened.

With Miller at the helm, the Riviera and its faithful following began to gain momentum. Not only were the rich businessmen frequenters of the club, but it also became a choice destination for the prom kids. Young and old thrilled to the glitzy shows featuring the finest talent of the day. Miller finally found his element, and nothing was going to stop him from exploiting it.

Ed Sullivan was a regular at the club. His *Toast of the Town* television show was booming, and still he found time to hang out backstage and chitchat with the star and the chorus girls. Lee Mortimer was another regular at the club. A columnist for the *New York Mirror*, a tabloid owned by William Randolph Hearst, Mortimer was the coauthor of a tell-all book series that had caused great consternation among the celebrities whose lives were exposed in each volume. Mortimer lost a $500,000 libel suit brought by a member of Congress, and his fifth marriage broke up over the attacks on Mortimer's character and lack of integrity. Both Sullivan and Mortimer wrote about the Riviera's shows and ambiances, letting the world know that the Riviera had raised the bar for every other nightclub in the country.

With the mambo craze sweeping the country, Miller jumped on that bandwagon and hired Pupi Campo and his orchestra. Pupi's aggregation consisted of about ten musicians, including conga, bongos and timbale drums. He would tear the house down with his version of "Mambo Jambo." Every hip couple who frequented nightclubs would take mambo dance lessons and then show up at the Riviera to show off their stuff. In a conversation in August 2011 with Dr. Carlos Campo, president of Regent University in Virginia and son of Pupi Campo, the authors learned that the former mambo king was well at age ninety-one and residing in Las Vegas.

Miller was no pushover when it came to sticking up for himself. There was an incident when he hired Milton Berle to appear at the Riviera. The William Morris Agency, the industry's premier booking agency, decided to have him appear at the Copacabana during the same period that he was appearing at the Riviera. Miller took serious umbrage to that and threatened suit. Berle bowed out of both deals, explaining that his new TV show, *Texaco Star Theater* on NBC, was requiring his full attention. Berle starred on the show for seven years and became the first major star of U.S. television. The William Morris Agency was the largest talent management company on both the East and West Coasts. It was owned in part by Jimmy "Blue Eyes" Alo, Meyer Lansky's chief assistant, who was loosely portrayed as Johnny Ola in the 1974 motion picture *Godfather Part II.*

THE STAGE IS SET

As Pupi Campo's Latin dance band ended its set with "Mambo Jambo," the hottest mambo tune of the day played by the hottest Latin band, happy and exhausted couples returned to their tables and banquettes to settle in to get ready to watch the show. The Riviera's lights began to dim. The round glass skylight roof that covered the entire dining room was silently raised, practically unnoticed, and slid away from view, leaving the dark blue summer night sky filled with stars. When the room was dark, twinkling lights streaming through the huge windows facing the George Washington Bridge added the finishing decorator's touch to what was going to be a magical moment.

The bandstand began to revolve, slowly exiting Pupi Campo's band and bringing to the front the Walter Nye show orchestra, made up of the best musicians that Musicians Local 526 out of Hudson County could provide. Off stage, Arty Johnson, the production singer, made an announcement in his deep baritone voice, "Good evening ladies and gentlemen. Bill Miller's Riviera proudly presents the Donn Arden–Ron Fletcher production of 'Bless All those Beautiful Girls.'" Walter Nye then counted (off mike) to his musicians: one and two and...down beat! Spotlights began zooming around the stage as the orchestra came to life. Tenor sax man Artie Frye led the four-sax section, along with three trumpets and two trombones, with Irwin Russo on drums. A piano player, an upright bass and Walter Nye out front leading the band burst into the up-tempo production number, "Bless All Those Beautiful Girls."

In time with the music's tempo, twelve gorgeous chorus girls, including Junior Jackson, Dusty Reale, Pat Cotton, Judy Tyler, Joy Skylar and others

Production singer Artie Johnson posing with the Riviera showgirls. *Courtesy of the Austin family collection.*

Bill Miller (left) with Milton Berle, Dean Martin, Jerry Lewis, Red Buttons, Phil Foster, Myron Cohen and others from in and out of show business. *Courtesy of the Fort Lee Historical Society.*

Above: Mambo band leader Pupi Campo with Danny Kaye and Jack Benny, who were among the top entertainers of the time. *Courtesy of the Fort Lee Historical Society.*

Left: Comedian Jackie Leonard in fine form sporting his famous Panama hat. *Courtesy of the Austin family collection.*

BEAUTIFUL **GIRLS**

MAR.
25c

K

LINDA
WILLIAMS
*Beauty
with Brains*
★
INSIDE STORY OF
BUNNY
YEAGER
★
GLAMOROUS
SHOWGIRLS
★
America's
Favorite
Model

JUNIOR
JACKSON

Right: Riviera showgirl Junior Jackson was also a favorite. *Courtesy of the Austin family collection.*

Below: The twelve Riviera showgirls posing in the wardrobe room. *Courtesy of the Austin family collection.*

Ballerina Nancy Crompton at
the Riviera. *Courtesy of the Fort
Lee Historical Society.*

Veteran Riviera showgirl Joy
Skylar. *Courtesy of the Austin
family collection.*

whose names are still etched in the history of the Riviera, began to quickstep onto the stage, doing the sensuous and "patented" Donn Arden Showgirl Walk. The walk, created by Arden, consisted of twisting the foot and swinging the pelvis forward. Donn would always say that if you twist the pelvis the right way and swing the torso, you get a revolve going that is just right. The girls' costumes, extremely tasteful, were designed to reveal almost every physical attribute they had. Donn Arden required that the girls had to be at least five feet, eight inches tall and have great legs and small, firm breasts. He insisted on displaying his showgirls in the best of taste, with their beautiful forms accentuated with little pillbox hats tilting perfectly on upswept hairdos. As they settled on their stage marks, their white elbow-length gloved hands placed on their hips, they posed motionless on the revolving dance floor as Arty Johnson sang his refrain. When the opening number ended, the girls quickstepped off the stage for their costume change for the next number.

Show business spectacles like this do not just happen—they take months and even years of planning. The lighting, the costumes, the musical arrangements, the stage engineering and the financial investment required are all necessary elements to complete the planning. It was in this area of show business that production partners Donn Arden and Ron Fletcher displayed their collected genius and that Bill Miller found his element. Miller knew that only the best would do when planning a show like this, and his first choice for production planning was Arden, a choreographer he knew through his booking agent days.

In an interview in 2011, the legendary Fluff LeCoque, a former Lido de Paris showgirl in the late 1940s who is the original and still current production manager for the Las Vegas Bally's Jubilee show (celebrating its thirtieth anniversary) said, "This show was created by Donn Arden. Donn was a genius that never got his full reward." In the interview, she explained that she was just a girl from Montana who sort of grew up in the state of Washington. As a teenager, she began her dancing career traveling through Europe, winding up in France in the line of the Lido de Paris show. Upon returning from Paris, she came to New York to meet with Donn Arden at his office. Fluff was immediately hired and sent to Ohio to do a Donn Arden show that was making the circuit of exclusive resorts and nightclubs in the Midwest.

Fluff said that during the time Bill Miller had engaged Donn Arden and Ron Fletcher to stage the Riviera show, Arden and Fletcher were in high demand throughout the United States. She went on to explain that Arden had a set pattern in staging his shows: "He would always have a handsome

Chorus dancer Janice Wallace shows the right look. *Courtesy of the Austin family collection.*

Riviera chorus dancer Elisa Jayne. *Courtesy of the Austin family collection.*

The Vagabonds knocking 'em dead! *Courtesy of the Austin family collection.*

Riviera showgirl
Dusty Reale had
her own following.
*Courtesy of the Austin
family collection.*

The Riviera chorus ready for the Betty Boop number. *Courtesy of the Austin family collection.*

production singer, and about twelve gorgeous girls. Donn would always choose beauty first and talent second."

Donn Arden was a dancer himself, born in 1917 in St. Louis, Missouri. By the time he was twenty, he had created his own dance troupes that performed in clubs in many cities. It was during this period that he met Bill Miller, the booking agent and former dancer. He and Bill became friends right away, with both having respect for each other's talent. It was Arden who insisted on holding ten- and twelve-hour rehearsals day after day until the chorus line was in perfect sync. It was during Arden's days at the Riviera in the early 1950s that the Chicago mob, which had invested heavily in Las Vegas to open the Desert Inn, noticed just how great the Riviera shows were and made Donn a lucrative offer that he chose not to pass up. Mobsters including Moe Dalitz, Morris Kleinman and Sam Tucker took points in the Desert Inn when owner Wilber Clark ran out of operating cash, and they wanted to make sure that their investment was protected. They needed a Donn Arden production to attract gamblers to the Desert Inn.

Much more of the Riviera chorus revealed. *Courtesy of the Austin family collection.*

By the late 1940s and early 1950s, Bill Miller had turned the big ship around, and the Riviera was showing a profit. The Riviera now set the standard for shows, and all other nightclub owners hoped to emulate. The Riviera became so popular that even some of the chorus girls became celebrities. Judy Tyler became Princess Summer Fall Winter Spring on *Howdy Doody with Buffalo Bob*, an early television show for children aired on Channel Five, then the Dumont Television Network. Images of Junior Jackson could be seen in fan magazines across the country, and Pat Cotton and others went to Las Vegas to star in shows that emulated the Parisian shows that featured chorus girls in tasteful nudity.

Although the Riviera became the proving ground for Donn Arden productions, Las Vegas ultimately became the site where Arden gained legendary status. With mob money behind him, he created shows in Vegas that are legendary to this day in the annals of show business history. For example, he created the sinking of the *Titanic* in the Bally's show "Jubilee" by flooding the stage with thousands of gallons of water. He was also the first to display on stage the bare breasts of chorus girls, a Las Vegas phenomenon.

Left: Pat Cotton, a Donn Arden dancer. *Courtesy of the Austin family collection.*

Below: Jack Cole's interpretive dance number. *Courtesy of the Austin family collection.*

At the Riviera, Arden's showgirls were all well rehearsed, and what they lacked in formal dance skills they more than made up for in beauty. Many gorgeous women auditioned for a spot in the Riviera's chorus line as a way to get some exposure in hopes of becoming noticed and making it in the movies or television. Their ages ranged between eighteen and twenty-five years. Some of the more ambitious and uninhibited would take on after-hours modeling jobs at art and photography studios to make ends meet. For living quarters, the girls would typically team up three or four at a time and rent inexpensive local apartments around the town of Fort Lee. It was not uncommon for a bevy of these beauties to swim in the saltwater pool at Palisades Amusement Park when they were not working at the club. If they were spotted by a photographer for the *New York Daily News*, their picture would be in the next morning's edition, which meant great publicity for the Riviera. However, on occasion, a chorus lovely would arrive at the Riviera in a new Cadillac wearing a full-length mink or sporting a Cartier diamond given to her by an admirer. Needless to say, stage door Johnnies, men who hung around waiting for a glimpse of the chorus, were never too far behind the girls as they made their daily trips to and from the Riviera.

Every show presented had a specific format that was basically a variety-type show. The show would always open with a production number featuring the showgirls and the production singer. Next came comedians like Jimmy Durante, Jackie Leonard, Zero Mostel, Henny Youngman, Jan Murray, Danny Thomas, Jack Carter, Phil Forster, Joey Bishop, Buddy Hackett, Dean Martin and Jerry Lewis, Milton Berle, Myron Cohen or Alan King. The list went on and on of the top banana comedians Bill Miller hired to entertain his customers.

Following the comedians, there was a ballroom dance team. The regulars included Marge and Gower Champion, the Cabots, the Zonys, Bambi Lynn and Rod Alexander and the Jack Cole Dancers. Miller would even book acrobats like Los Gatos, the Romanos, novelty acts like ventriloquist Paul Winchell and Jerry Mahoney, Johnny Puleo and the Harmonica Rascals. But there was one group in particular that caught Bill Miller's fancy, and it wasn't a dance team or acrobatic team. It happened to be a small group of musicians called the Vagabonds: Angelo, Al, Tillio and Pete. They were great musicians and also great comedians. There was something about using a small group of musicians that instilled an idea in Miller's head that would come to fruition years later when he created the lounge act in Las Vegas.

Miller realized that a small group of talented musicians could do a whole show and save a great deal of expense for the business's management while doing a fantastic job of entertaining the customers. Not only were "combos," as they were called, easier to manage and could work small rooms or big rooms, but the cost was also far less. There was a flexibility and utility within a group like that set the wheels turning in Miller's head. Years later, long after the Riviera closed and Miller went to Las Vegas, he immediately hired Louis Prima and Keely Smith, along with Sam Butera and the Witnesses, for a long-term contract at the Sahara Hotel's Casbah Lounge. They became Las Vegas's first lounge acts, an idea that made Miller a legend on the Vegas Strip.

Engaging the headliners became the most difficult aspect of setting up the Riviera shows. Headliners were booked sometimes years in advance. The chorus line was an in-house group. The ballroom dancers made the rounds in shows across the country, but most were only limited to entertaining in nightclubs, with the exception of Marge and Gower Champion, who also starred in motion pictures. The headliners were a completely different story. They were usually singers who also had multiple careers as movie actors and actresses, recording artists and TV personalities; they also made product endorsements. Each aspect of their careers required scheduling, with plenty of lead time. They were all traveling internationally as well, so booking a top name a year or two in advance was a risky business. Although stars might be popular in 1949, who could predict that their popularity would continue in the coming year or two. Therefore, a contractual commitment of $5,000 or $10,000 per week for an appearance that would not happen until sometime in the future was a speculative decision. The question always arose as to what is the present worth of a future benefit. Miller predicted the continuing popularity of blue chip acts and took calculated risks in signing contracts for performances for dates in the future.

When the production number finished, the comedian would come on stage, do his or her shtick and bond with the audience. Performers like Jimmy Durante had universal appeal and attracted all manner of ethnic groups. Others, like Myron Cohen and Zero Mostel, packed the place with Jewish patrons. Red Buttons, with his "Ho Ho He He" routine, also did very well. Phil Foster held court with the Italians when he would do his routine about "I shoulda ducked." Alan King was just a kid when he would do his act talking about his family.

The audiences for these shows were always packed with celebrities. People like Sugar Ray Robinson, the champion prizefighter, would routinely come to the Riviera. New York Yankees slugger Mickey Mantle would usually be on the scene after games, hanging out backstage or in the barbershop being

Above: The Riviera chorus dancing a new number. *Courtesy of the Fort Lee Historical Society.*

Right: Sammy Davis Jr. and the champ, Sugar Ray Robinson. *Courtesy of the Fort Lee Historical Society.*

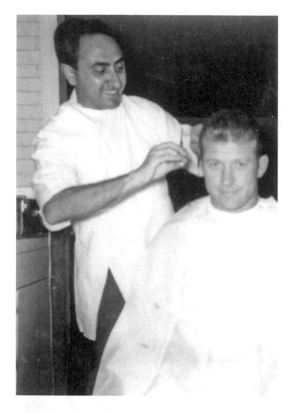

"The Mick," Mickey Mantle, having his hair cut by Rocky Vitetta at the Riviera. *Courtesy of the Rocky Vitetta collection.*

Movie star Jane Mansfield received a lot of attention from the Riviera's captains. *Courtesy of the Fort Lee Historical Society.*

Fort Lee's Johnny Puleo
and his Harmonica
Rascals. *Courtesy of the
Fort Lee Historical Society.*

attended to by the Riviera barber Rocky Vitetta. Miller loved it when athletes
would show up because they became added attractions for the customers.
Joe DiMaggio was always surrounded by show business stars and made the
news columns the next day. Usually the athletes would be happy to sign
autographs. When Sinatra performed at the Riviera, Ava Gardner would be
in the audience, and Jane Mansfield and friends would arrive for a late show.

As the waiters, busboys, cigarette girls and photography girls scurried
through the audience during the shows, the word from the boss was to keep
it quiet. Sal Negrone, a local busboy working his way through law school,
would take time out and stand by the swinging doors to the kitchen to enjoy
a moment or two of listening to his favorite comedian, Jimmy Durante.
Sal then would get back to the task of cleaning off the tables and lugging
full trays of dirty dishes down the stairs to the kitchen. In later years, Sal
Negrone became a prominent attorney in New York City. Diane Rockefeller,
a gorgeous redhead from Englewood, would go from table to table, strolling
through the audience in a French maid outfit and carrying her white tray
for selling cigarettes. The carhops, after parking all the cars, would find a
comfortable tree outside and climb it to watch the star-studded Riviera show.

Coauthor Tom Austin and his mother, Mildred, at a table close to the Riviera's stage. *Courtesy of the Austin family collection.*

Something little-known to the average person was the generosity the stars bestowed on the people who helped make their appearance a success. It was customary for the star of the show to give lavish gifts to the people who aided them during their appearances at the club. For example, Peggy Lee would give beautiful silver cigarette lighters, and Tony Martin would give rings and cash—no one was forgotten. Considering that stars were making weekly salaries in the $5,000 range when the average person was earning perhaps $50 per week made it a little easier for the star to be generous, but nevertheless most of the headliners seem to have shared that attribute.

As the preliminary acts were finishing their routines, the audience was well primed in anticipation of seeing the headliner who was about to go on. The reporters and critics in the audience took out their pads and pencils and scribbled notes as to what was going to go into their columns on the following day. Theatrical agents like Bill Ficks (the Ames Brothers' manager), representing other acts currently appearing at the Riviera, would leave their seats and jump to another table to pitch their clients to some out-of-town club owner in to catch the Riviera show. Sugar daddies enjoying a night on the town with much younger women, seemingly young enough to be their daughters, ordered the finest champagne and caviar, more to impress the girl than to enjoy it. Husbands and wives celebrating anniversaries were all smiles as the waiter Lou Gallo would gift an orchid corsage from Paterson's Orchids in Bergenfield to the lady, compliments of Bill Miller. Young couples celebrating an office promotion on their first big night out since the baby was born would sip their drinks nervously and wonder how their babysitter at home was doing. Mob guys and the women who loved them slouched back comfortably, obviously used to this electrified atmosphere. A young boy about twelve years old sat at a ringside table with a pretty, well-dressed woman in her thirties. Who were they? The boy looked in bright-eyed wonder at everything that was taking place in the room as the headwaiter ordered two club sandwiches and Cokes to be brought to their table.

The room once again darkened.

HERE COME THE
HEADLINERS

The Riviera never fell short on booking the greatest names of the day to headline the club's shows. *Billboard* magazine reported in April 1951 that the lineup of stars to grace the Riviera stage for the summer season included Billy Daniels, Danny Thomas, Tony Martin, Jackie Miles and Lena Horne.

Other names that filled the bill on successive occasions read like the who's who of superstars. Miller's army of talent never stopped coming, just like the customers: Frank Sinatra, Sammy Davis Jr. with the Will Masten Trio, Joel Gray, Jane Frohman, Victor Borge, Joey Bishop, Dean Martin and Jerry Lewis, Peggy Lee, Tony Arden, Martha Ray, Vic Damone, Jimmy Durante—all at their height in show business, headlined at the Riviera.

One interesting aspect of the Riviera programming was that Bill Miller would manage to fill the house with at least two shows a night, whereas the Copacabana would only have one show. Lena Horne, a major black vocalist fresh from appearing in a string of Hollywood motion pictures, said that if Bill Miller suddenly decided to put on three shows a night when she was appearing there, she'd have none of it.

When Miller took over the Riviera in 1945, the first thing he did was hire a female disc jockey named Bee Kalmus to put on a radio show from 1:00 a.m. to 2:00 a.m. that emanated from the Riviera's lounge over the call letters WHN. The time had come for Miller to let the world know that his Riviera was America's Showplace and that it would take second place to none. To do that, he had to have the hottest headliner that money could buy: Tony Martin. To really demonstrate Miller's intention of having the

The sensational Bambi Lynn and Rod Alexander. *Courtesy of the Austin family collection.*

Jan Murray, the great funnyman. *Courtesy of the Austin family collection.*

Jack Carter, one of early television's most enduring stars. *Courtesy of the Austin family collection.*

Mr. Billy Daniels: "That old black magic." *Courtesy of the Austin family collection.*

Jane Frohman sings, "I walk alone." *Courtesy of the Austin family collection.*

Frank Sinatra and Bill Miller with the Riviera showgirls. *Courtesy of the Fort Lee Historical Society.*

Riviera recognized as superior over all other nightclubs, including the world-renowned Copacabana in Manhattan, Miller decided that he would pay Martin $10,000 per week. That was a kingly sum, twice as much as Martin was paid by Jules Podell at the Copa. Miller said later that he wished that the Riviera had rubber walls so he could pack in more people.

Year after year, the Riviera shows were spectacular. Because the club was only open from April through October, in addition to one extra night (New Year's Eve), the crowds of patrons were kept impatient and begging for the next extravaganza that Miller was planning due to the barrage of publicity created by Ed Winer and Seth Babits, Miller's publicity agents. The headliner for the opening of the 1953 season was Vic Damone. Vic had just finished his active duty in the army and was looking forward to returning to the stage. On that bill were Marge and Gower Champion and comedian Joey Bishop. Of course, the Donn Arden–Ron Fletcher chorus line was well rehearsed and ready to go as well.

As the Walter Nye orchestra opened with the number made famous by Benny Goodman, "Let's Dance," Marge and Gower Champion, the nation's premier dance team, took to the floor. In the audience was a couple that came to see the Champions that night. They were Bill Warfield, the black entertainer who sang "Ol' Man River" in the original Broadway musical *Show Boat*, and his date, Leontine Price, the Metropolitan Opera star.

As the Champions finished their opening number, their piano accompanist, Richard Pribor, set the tempo for the next tune, "Time on My Hands." As the dance team floated effortlessly through that number, the members of the audience were on their feet in appreciation.

In 2011, the authors interviewed Marge Champion, at age ninety-one. She explained that Bill Warfield and Leontine Price were close friends of hers and Gower's and that they came to the Riviera to say farewell, as they were scheduled to travel to the Soviet Union to open in the new George Gershwin opera *Porgy and Bess*.

Marge also explained that back in 1953, it was not common to see black people in the all-white audiences of places like the Riviera. She knew that everyone was welcome at the Riviera, but it was unusual, except for internationally renowned celebrities, for black patrons to be present. She went on to say that although the couple might have felt uncomfortable, they didn't show it because Bill was so smitten with Leontine that he could not take his eyes off her, and he was oblivious to what was going on around them. The Champions finished their repertoire of songs that included "County Fair," "Margie" and "Meeting Time" and then left the stage to thunderous applause.

Arty Johnson, the voice behind the Riviera's production numbers. *Courtesy of the Austin family collection.*

Comedian Joey Bishop before he was drafted into the "Rat Pack." *Courtesy of the Austin family collection.*

To Tom.
Best wishes
Marge Gower Champion

Marge and Gower Champion, together since high school. *Courtesy of the Austin family collection.*

The next performer was Joey Bishop, billed as the "unhappy humorist." Joey, in his inimitable way, had the crowd rolling with his dry, inoffensive, quick-witted humor as he strolled around doing his imitation of Ted Lewis, of "Me and My Shadow," fame with his silk hat and clarinet. Once, while Bishop was appearing at the Riviera, Marilyn Monroe entered the club. Everyone in the audience ignored Bishop and focused on Marilyn. To regain the audience's attention, Bishop said, "Hey Honey, didn't I tell you to wait in the truck?" The place went wild. When Joey finished his routine, the crowd was all warmed up and ready for the headliner: popular vocalist Vic Damone.

As the Walter Nye orchestra laid down the intro of "Will You Still Be Mine," the audience didn't realize that Vic's conductor and accompanist replaced the house pianist in the Nye orchestra. Vic's accompanist was none other than Burt Bacharach, who went on to compose dozens of hit songs.

As the chorus line girls came out in their gorgeous costumes, Vic strolled casually out onto the stage wearing a supercool light-gray tuxedo. The

Vic Damone, one of the great ones, the best of the best. *Courtesy of the Austin family collection.*

Victor Borge, the funny concert pianist. *Courtesy of the Austin family collection.*

women in the audience began to lose control as Vic so adeptly voiced the words to the Tom Adair/Matt Dennis tune "Will You Still Be Mine":

When cabs don't drive around the park
No windows light the summer dark
When love has lost its secret spark
Will you still be mine?

When he got to the part of the song called the "release" or the "bridge," the lyrics so related to the setting that evening that the audience burst out in applause:

When moonlight on the Hudson's not romancy
And spring no longer turns a young mans fancy

With the showgirls dancing around him, he continued:

When glamour girls have lost their charms
And sirens just mean false alarms
When lovers heed no call to arms
Will you still be mine?

The crowd went wild. Some members of the audience were on their feet, applauding as the chorus left the stage. Next Vic sang "April in Portugal," written by James Kennedy and Raul Ferrao. Vic at the time had a huge hit on his hands with this tune, and the audience knew it. When he finished the tune, he had the audience in the palm of his hand. The lights grew dim; the spotlight shined only on Vic's face as he went into the wartime favorite, "Where or When." The room with a thousand patrons was silent as he sang the emotional lyrics:

It seems we stood and talked like this before
We looked at each other in the same way then
But I can't remember where or when

The audience again reacted with joy and applause, and Vic followed with up-tempo songs like "Gypsy in My Soul." The audience loved it all, and at the back of the cavernous room stood "the boss," Bill Miller, among the waiter captains with a huge grin on his face, enjoying every minute of it just like his customers. Every show was like this one, every detail taken care of, but of course it worked because the audience was experiencing the best musical talent of the day.

The Tony Martin show in June 1953 featured the dance team of Bambi Lynn and Rod Alexander, as well as comedian Jackie Leonard. Tony, having established himself with Bill Miller as early as 1947, had become a regular at the Riviera. His following was unbelievable. Tony's fans were blue chip customers, and they spent lavishly. The Riviera was booked to capacity for every show, and Miller was forced to put on three shows per night, which was agreed to by Tony Martin, the most popular vocalist in America.

Tony's real name was Alvin Morris, and he was born in San Francisco, California, in 1913. Although most people thought that he was Italian, and he didn't disagree, he was really born to Jewish immigrant parents. As a kid, he learned to play the saxophone. That instrument was actually his ticket to a musical career. When he was a teenager at Oakland Technical High School, he joined his first real band, of local orchestra leader Tom Gerun, as a sax player. Coincidently, in that same band was another local boy, who played the clarinet. His name was Woody Herman. Herman played the clarinet and went on to establish himself as a band leader of renown during the big band era of the 1930s and 1940s.

After graduating from Saint Mary's College near his home in Oakland, California, Tony went to Hollywood to try and find a job in films. He changed his name to Tony Martin at this time. Martin quickly became known in Hollywood due to his great looks and personality. He signed with Twentieth Century Fox and then Metro-Goldwyn-Mayer. In 1941, he was featured in a Marx Brothers film called *The Big Store*. In that film, he performed and recorded the song "Tenement Symphony," written by Hal Borne, who then became Tony's lifelong musical director.

When Tony appeared at the Riviera, cars would literally be backed up to the next town of Englewood Cliffs. Tony was known

Henny Youngman: "Take my wife…please!"
Courtesy of the Austin family collection.

99

for always wearing the most fabulous tuxedos. He was tall, dark, slender and handsome, and therefore it was no surprise when Tony became the model for the After Six brand of tuxedos.

In his appearances at the Riviera, Tony always wore a straw skimmer hat that, back in the 1940s and early 1950s, was deemed to be so chic. The skimmer was also worn by Harry Richman, Desi Arnaz, Pupi Campo, Maurice Chevalier, W.C. Fields and even the ultra-popular and handsome Gene Kelly in the 1952 film *Singin' in the Rain*. The skimmer was worn with everything from casual clothes to tuxedos. When an attractive man tilted that flat-top straw hat over his left eye, women would go wild, and that was the effect that Tony had on the ladies when he wore the hat on stage.

Once again, it was show time, and Tony performed to a packed house. Over the years, Tony performed at Riviera at least seven or eight times. The chorus line came on and got the audience in a happy mood. Fat Jackie Leonard went on and broke up the house with his almost off-color humor, and then Tony went on and tore down the house down with "La Vie En Rose." The waiters, captains, cigarette girls and photography girls all got big tips, and everyone went home happy. Tony was a generous man and gave lavish tips to everyone who helped him with his performance. He married dancer Cyd Charisse, one of the motion picture industry's most beautiful women. Their sixty-five-year marriage ended in 2008 with her death. Charisse was born in Amarillo, Texas, and her real name was Tula Ellice Finklea. She went on to costar with the great dancers Fred Astaire and Gene Kelly in many significant motion pictures.

When Sammy Davis Jr. appeared at the Riviera with the Will Masten Trio, made up of his uncle, Will, and his father, it was Sammy who stole the show. Sammy Davis Jr. was only a kid back then, but he could tap-dance like nobody's business, play the drums, twirl six-guns in holsters and sing like a bird on stage. Sammy could do it all. He attracted lots of athletes who wanted to see him perform. Sugar Ray Robinson, considered by the Associated Press the greatest boxer of all time, became a regular at the club when Sammy was performing. Everyone knew when Sugar Ray had arrived because he would drive his signature pink Cadillac filled with a carload of his friends from the newspaper and prizefighting worlds.

Dean Martin would be in the audience when Sammy was in town, as would Joey Bishop and Frank Sinatra—all the guys who also played Skinny D'Amato's 500 Club in Atlantic City. Like the Riviera, the 500 Club also was known to have its own secret card room long before gambling casinos were legal in Atlantic City. In the late 1940s and early 1950s, these guys were

Maitre d's and captains ready for an evening at the Riviera. *Courtesy of the Fort Lee Historical Society.*

considered the new kids on the block, but they all went on to have fantastic successes. They also remained close friends and later were known as the "Rat Pack," which also included Peter Lawford and some associate female members from the motion picture industry.

Whenever Frank Sinatra would appear at the Riviera, there was no shortage of excitement. On one occasion, it was reported that Frank brought his new girlfriend, the glamorous and mysterious film star Ava Gardner, to the club. Everything was fine until Marilyn Maxwell arrived. Marilyn was a gorgeous movie actress and former girlfriend of Frank's. While Marilyn was seated at ringside and enjoying the show, Ava, at another table, began to think that Frank was singing love songs to his old flame. Ava was known to have had an explosive temperament, and she jumped up out of her seat, knocking over a chair while shouting a few expletives, and rushed out of the club. Frank was devastated and eventually caught up with Ava in Hollywood weeks later and set things right.

In 1952, Frank Sinatra's career was on a downward slide. His voice was overworked, and he was losing his touch with his singing. Frank's stock was dropping, and he was the first to realize it. This occurred after years of popularity, especially with young female fans known as "bobbysoxers." Recognizing the fact that he needed to land the big one to refresh his popularity, Frank went after the part of Maggio in the movie *From Here to Eternity.* In her book about Frank Sinatra, Kitty Kelly explained that the studio did not even want to have Sinatra test for the part, but after Ava Gardner, Frank's wife at the time, intervened and asked the wife of studio head Harry Cohn to give Frank a screen test, she did and the test was arranged. The screen test went so well that Frank beat out Eli Wallach for the part. After he completed shooting his segment of the movie in May 1953, he decided to take a tour of Europe for a few months to see if his voice would return. It did, and upon his return in August to the United States, Bill Miller signed him to play the Riviera later that year.

Earlier that spring, Frank had recorded the song "From Here to Eternity," and his record was taking off like a rocket ship. In November 1953, Frank was set to appear at the Riviera. Miller once again made the right call and timed it perfectly. Miller rolled out the red carpet and invited every celebrity

Frank Sinatra and a Korean war hero chat about the film *From Here to Eternity. Courtesy of the Austin family collection.*

Eddie Fisher came to the Riviera to hear Sinatra sing. Fisher headlined in the Riviera's closing show. *Courtesy of the Austin family collection.*

on his list to attend Frank's opening. The joint was packed to the rafters when he opened.

The cool November night was brisk and clear, as was Sinatra's voice. The room was filled to capacity. People started arriving earlier than usual that night for the 8:00 p.m. show. At 6:00 p.m., the Serpentine Bar was packed three and four deep with early arrivals hoping to be seated at ringside tables. Something in the air was indeed special that night—even the cars that arrived at the Riviera were different than usual. Instead of the brightly colored convertibles usually seen in the parking lot, a long line of black Cadillac sedans and limousines lined up at the entrance like sentries awaiting the arrival of the king. That night, the audience was made up mainly of Frank's friends and other well-wishers. Sure, mobsters were there, too. Frank had a happy history with them. Everyone was there to welcome Frankie home. It was said later that there were so many minks and ermines in the room that it looked like a furrier's convention. Those who were graced with ringside tables that night were the envy of everyone else in the room.

Sammy Davis Jr., with Riviera barber Rocky Vitetta at his right, along with other Riviera staff and showgirls. *Courtesy of the Rocky Vitetta collection.*

The Riviera's menu that night included:

SPECIALTIES OF THE HOUSE

Special BBQ Spare Ribs	*2.00*
White Meat Chicken Chow Mein with	
Mushrooms, Water Chestnuts and Bamboo Shoots	*4.00*
Chinese Pepper Steak with Mushrooms	*4.00*
Prime Roast Beef	*5.00*
Sliced Roast Turkey or Chicken	*3.25*
Chilled Shrimp Cocktail	*2.50*
Fresh Whole Maine Lobster	*4.25*

The waiters tried mightily to keep up with the happy, free-spending patrons, who didn't skimp on what they ordered. The feast was on and the Riviera was jumping. The bar and food orders were turning over so fast that the busboys were instructed to dump the full trays of dirty dishes through an open window located just outside the swinging doors to the dining room, over the side of the cliff. This wasn't an environmentally sound practice, and today it would engender a legal complaint and possibly criminal prosecution, but in the 1950s no one was watching.

When things settled down and the crowd quieted, Frank's musical conductor pointed his finger at the orchestra, gave two beats and said, "Do it." As if by magic, the band kicked in big time as the opening bars to "I Get a Kick Out of You" ushered Frank onto the stage. Frank took it right to them that night in his unique style. The crowd became mesmerized by his delivery and verve. "You Go to My Head," "My Funny Valentine" and "One for My Baby"—on and on the tunes were delivered, one better and more solid than the other. During the show, Frank introduced Harold Arlen, who was in the audience. Arlen, one of the great composers of that era, wrote "One for My Baby," a Sinatra signature song. Eddie Fisher was also in the audience that night and was introduced by Frank.

Sinatra's new arranger, Nelson Riddle, a young man from Wyckoff, New Jersey, along with his other Capital records arrangers, Gordon Jenkins and Billy May, seemed to be the missing links that Frank needed in order to add that perfect musical background punctuation to his voice. Frank's rendition of "They Can't Take That Away From Me" sort of summed up the evening.

The 1953 movie *From Here to Eternity*, adapted from the James Jones novel, was destined to be an Academy Award winner, with Sinatra winning an Oscar as Best Supporting Actor. Frank had returned to his rightful place as "King of the Hill," and no one could take that away from him. The kid from Hoboken took the Riviera by storm that night, never to slump again.

When the show was over, the crowd tumbled out into the parking lot. It was surprising that no one wanted to leave right away. According to an observer, the crowd just hung around like kids on a street corner. The night

Alan King, the hilarious storyteller. *Courtesy of the Austin family collection.*

105

air was indeed cold by 1:00 a.m., but that didn't seem to bother the crowd. The women bundled up under their furs and talked with one another. The men collared up their overcoats, pulled the brims down on their fedora hats and just stood around congratulating one another on the experience they all had just shared. The chauffeurs, with hands in their pockets and cigarettes dangling from their lips, leaned back on the fenders of cars, waiting for something to happen. The Riviera's chorus girls just stood by the stage door watching the goings-on, afraid that if they left they would miss something as the happy crowd just seemed to hang out and wait.

That night, celebrities, athletes, mobsters and just average patrons all hung out together on the front steps and in the Riviera's parking lot and celebrated the colossal return of a local icon. Frank was always perceived to be a guy from everyone's neighborhood, and even though he had gone through the roughest time in his career a few years before, he was back on track and everybody that night watched him prove it. A little while later, all eyes turned to the stage door as four men leading the way pushed past the crowd of chorus girls blocking the stage entrance, and Frank Sinatra exited the building wearing a gray checked overcoat with a white Turkish towel wrapped around his neck. The crowd, as if on cue, began applauding and whistling as Frank turned and looked at them, seemingly shocked by what was happening. This was not the typical response the young bobbysoxer girls had given him years before. This time, the guys were cheering for him as well. If Frank ever had any doubts about how his fans would receive him while attempting to make his comeback, those doubts could be put to rest for good.

Gus Grossman's Fort Lee Diner was packed with the fall-out crowd from the Riviera until the early hours of the morning. No one wanted the party to end, and it didn't. The talk as the sun began to rise in the east was all about Sinatra's great performance and how it would never be forgotten.

Bill Miller's dream of owning the greatest nightclub in the world also became reality that night. Every syndicated newspaper columnist, every movie tabloid and every fan magazine, along with every radio and TV news station, filled the airwaves with the news of Frank's successful return to his singing career, and it happened at the Riviera.

Ed Sullivan, the nationally syndicated *New York Daily News* columnist, was a regular at the Riviera, always in search of some new talent for his CBS *Toast of the Town* show on Sunday evenings at 8:00 p.m., sponsored by Lincoln Mercury. His show ran for twenty-three years on CBS, the longest-running variety show ever presented on national television. Sullivan helped the Riviera immensely by introducing performers on the TV show and prefixing their introduction by mentioning that the act "headlined at Bill Miller's Riviera over in New Jersey." Ed was not always the best at remembering the names of the people he was introducing. On one occasion, he introduced Victor Borge this way: "Ladies and gentleman, let's give a nice New York welcome to a guy who just had a successful run at Bill Miller's Riviera in New Jersey…Let's hear it for Victor Bor-gee." Another time, while introducing three New York Yankees in his audience, he asked the players to come to the stage, and then he said to one of them, "Which one are you?"

Headliner Tony Martin chats with captain Bruno before the show. *Courtesy of the Fort Lee Historical Society.*

No one cared very much about a mispronounced word or an errant slip of the tongue in those days, and of course everything was live TV back then and the teleprompter had not been invented yet. So Ed Sullivan and others like him just went on and did their best, and as long as Bill Miller's name and the Riviera were mentioned, all was well at America's Showplace.

What's so interesting about the reputation of the Riviera is that when Bill Miller's Riviera is mentioned, it invokes smiles and memories from anyone who remembers it. The Riviera set high standards for the great showplaces in Las Vegas that followed in its footsteps. It is safe to say that every act that appeared at the Riviera also appeared in Las Vegas and, eventually, in Havana. The network of clubs, gambling casinos and luxury hotels that ran along the East Coast to Cuba and eventually to Las Vegas was tied together by secret relationships that were only whispered about. Meyer Lansky, Jimmy Alo and probably countless public officials, bankers and attorneys worked quietly behind the scenes to move the millions in cash from illegal operations to safe havens on offshore islands and into well-known and legitimate businesses.

THE "BOYS" ARE
BACK IN TOWN

According to Al Austin, security officer at the Riviera, from the moment Bill Miller took over the club from Ben Marden in 1947, the U.S. government continued to take a special interest in that secret gambling room on the top floor of the Riviera. The insider's question was: "Will Miller reopen Marden's gaming room or won't he?" Although everything was kept quiet as far as the government was concerned, a young United States senator, Estes Kefauver from Monroe County, Tennessee, who had been elected to the Senate in 1948, was trying to make a name for himself and was hellbent on going after organized crime in the United States to do so. Kefauver, wearing his trademark black-framed eyeglasses, was a model of patience when he questioned the powerful hoodlums the committee subpoenaed to testify. The hearings made for dramatic television watching. Television was still in its infancy, and for the first time, real criminals and their stories were seen in millions of homes on black-and-white television sets. Most of the watchers learned a new word. The mafia was real and powerful, even if FBI director J. Edgar Hoover denied it until his dying day.

It was no secret that the Federal Bureau of Investigation was making nightly treks to Fort Lee to park its unmarked cars at the foot of the Riviera lot, trying to observe the comings and goings of local gangsters Joe Adonis, Willie Moretti and even the big crime boss Frank Costello, all of whom were frequent visitors to the Riviera. When Frank Sinatra appeared at the Riviera, the Fischetti brothers from Chicago always seemed to be in attendance.

When Charlie "Trigger Happy" Fischetti and his brother, Rocco, arrived in town for the Riviera shows, there was a mystique surrounding them.

Everyone at the Riviera was on high alert for their arrival. The Fischetti boys were first cousins of Al Capone, and according to reports, they took turns acting as drivers for Capone. In 1932, Rocco was arrested with Meyer Lansky, Lucky Luciano and Paul Ricca at the Congress Hotel in Chicago during an important mob meeting. Some people on the inside of organized crime claimed that it was the Fischetti brothers who received the contract for the hit on Bugsy Siegel. Siegel was credited with being one of the first to realize the potential of Las Vegas, which at the time was an air force field in the desert. He somehow knew that Nevada was ready for legalized gambling and other vices. When the United States Senate Special Committee to Investigate Crime in Interstate Commerce convened in Washington and called in the Fischettis to testify on their involvement in organized crime, Charlie Fischetti unexpectedly died only nine days after they turned themselves in—and, more importantly, before he could testify.

Another Riviera regular was the notorious Willie Moretti. According to author Anthony Bruno in his book *Frank Sinatra and the Mob*, Moretti bragged that it was he and two of his associates who rescued Frank Sinatra from an unfair contract with band leader Tommy Dorsey. Sinatra was under a lifetime personal services contract with Dorsey, and Sinatra wanted to cancel it because Dorsey would take a large percentage of Sinatra's earnings. The story has it that Sinatra's settlement with Dorsey in the event that the contract was cancelled amounted to Sinatra paying Dorsey and his agent a sum equal to 43 percent of his income for life. Moretti, who a few years before had taken the young Sinatra under his wing, visited Dorsey and made him an offer he could not refuse. Frank Sinatra always denied that Moretti's intervention helped in having his contract with Dorsey cancelled, but according to a reporter from *American Mercury* magazine, Dorsey admitted that he had been visited by three men "who talked out of the corners of their mouths" and ordered him to sign Sinatra's release or else.

Frank Costello was about fifty years old back in 1951 when he would come to the Riviera, and he had become tired of the life he led. In 1936, Frank first became the acting boss, appointed by Charles "Lucky" Luciano, who was then serving a term up in Danemora Prison by the Canadian border. At that time, Luciano also appointed Vito Genovese to serve as the under boss. In the late 1940s, Genovese fled to Italy when an impending arrest warrant was issued accusing him of murder, which left Frank Costello in total charge—a responsibility that Costello handled very well.

Costello was known as a gentleman who used his brain instead of his muscles to rule the rackets. When Genovese returned from Italy after eight

Security officer Al Austin with some of the Riviera staff. *Courtesy of the Austin family collection.*

years of hiding, he observed how strong Costello had become thanks to his affiliations with Joe Adonis and Albert Anastasia and how his wealth and political power protected him from arrest and prosecution. When the Kefauver Committee was organized to expose crime and criminals in the United States, it was recognized that Frank Costello was probably the most powerful mob figure in the country. Vito Genovese, although friendly with Costello in the early days, felt strongly that the time had come to get rid of Costello, who was a public figure with whom the press and public had a fascination.

Late one evening, when Costello returned to his Manhattan apartment from a night on the town, a gunman approached him from behind and exclaimed, "Hey, this is for you Frank," firing a point-blank shot at Costello's head. When Costello heard the words spoken by the gunman to his rear, he turned his head slightly, thus causing the bullet to miss a direct hit. Instead, the bullet encircled his head just under the skin and harmlessly fell to the floor, exiting from over his left ear. The hit man was later identified as

Vincent "The Chin" Gigante, an ex-prizefighter who was also the driver for Vito Genovese.

At Gigante's trial for the attempted assassination, when asked if the person who shot at him was in the courtroom, Frank Costello, after looking around the room, replied that he could not positively identify the person who shot him, thus letting Vincent off the hook. Legend has it that the Chin approached Costello after the trial and thanked him for not fingering him.

The assassination attempt was a life-changing experience for Frank Costello. At this point, it became obvious to people close to him that Costello had lost his will to rule the mob. It was even said that he began seeing a psychiatrist due to depression. This theme was carried out decades later in the hit HBO series *The Sopranos*, in which crime boss Tony Soprano enters into a lengthy therapeutic relationship with a psychiatrist for treatment of depression. Costello subsequently negotiated a deal with Vito Genovese that, in effect, allowed him to live untouched if he stepped down from power and handed his authority totally over to Genovese. In addition, Costello was ordered by Genovese to relinquish his points in the Copacabana nightclub in New York, which took him out of the nightclub scene in Manhattan. The terms of the deal were obviously accepted by both men because Costello died peacefully in his sleep at the age of eighty-two.

When word got out that the United States Senate Special Committee to Investigate Crime in Interstate Commerce was scheduled to hold hearings on organized crime across the nation, the card room (or "dice barn," as it was called) in the Riviera roof never did seem to open anymore. By the time the Kefauver hearings in Washington were underway, anyone who had anything to do with aiding or abetting gambling, drugs, prostitution, loan sharking and racketeering was feeling the heat. Even the inside guys in the mob began distrusting one another. Things came to a head on October 4, 1951, when Willie Moretti and a few of his friends met at Joe's Elbow Room in Cliffside on the Fort Lee town line to have breakfast. Before coffee was served, two of his so called pals pulled out .38-caliber pistols and shot Willie at point-blank range in the head, killing him instantly. It was presumed that Willie's lack of self-control and outbursts that resulted in his walking out of the Kefauver hearings during his testimony had created too much negative attention and compromised the "omertà" (code of silence) by which the mob lived.

Immediately following that incident, the tension around Fort Lee became so thick that you could slice it with a pair of wire cutters. The newspapers were filled with the story of Moretti's murder, and the pressure was really on from prosecutors and police. Ironically, two days later on October 6, 1951, Fort Lee police chief Fred Stengel, who had allegedly been involved in supplying protection for Adonis's gambling operations, was found dead from a gunshot wound to the head near the Madonna Cemetery in Fort Lee—his death, while suspicious, was ruled a suicide.

There is an old saying, "Any publicity is good publicity," and that probably held true for the Riviera. With Fort Lee's notorious residents filling the papers every day, the public had the perception that the Riviera was a part of it. Maybe it was or maybe it wasn't. Whatever the case, business at the Riviera was booming.

According to FBI files, in 1951 Fort Lee resident and notorious gangster Albert Anastasia was feuding with New York's Mangano crime family, which later became known as the Gambino family. Vincent Mangano suddenly disappeared, and his brother, Phil Mangano, was found murdered. At that point, Anastasia was reported to have claimed immediate control of the Mangano family. When a subsequent meeting of the five New York crime families was held, Frank Costello backed Anastasia's claim that Mangano had been out to kill him and that any action taken by Albert Anastasia, including murder and kidnapping, was an act of self-defense. The crime bosses accepted Anastasia's position on the matter and honored his claim, thus endorsing his position as boss.

Anastasia lived in a splendid Spanish-style home in Fort Lee overlooking the Hudson River, with views of Manhattan's West Side. While Anastasia lived like a gentleman within his gated compound, he was actually a psychopath and a murderer. He and fellow racketeer Louis "Lepke" Buchalter, a borderline personality, headed the contract killing organization known as Murder Inc. They assigned their staff members to carry out killings ordered by the Commission, the ruling body of the national crime syndicate. It's estimated that Murder Inc. chalked up five hundred murders that were mostly not solved. Neither Anastasia nor Buchalter were prosecuted for these crimes. However, Buchalter was executed in New York's Sing Sing prison on March 5, 1944, for the murder of a candy store owner over a private matter.

Albert Anastasia strolled into Manhattan's Park Sheridan Hotel for his usual haircut, shave and shoeshine on October 25, 1957. The crime boss was cheerful and unconcerned about his own safety. He sat in the first chair for service from his regular barber, who covered Anastasia with a stripped cotton cloth to protect his clothing. A few moments later, two men with masks covering their faces burst into the barbershop, pushing the barber aside. They opened fire and hit Anastasia numerous times, killing him as he attempted to get out of the chair. The killers were not apprehended, and the case remains open to this day. Anastasia's palatial home was sold to comedian Buddy Hackett, who loved the property and wasn't bothered by its history.

Retired New York Police Department lieutenant Joseph Coffey, former head of the New York State Organized Crime Task Force, commented during an interview years later: "Everyone knew Bill Miller's Riviera was all mobbed up. Most nights, the mobsters held court at the ringside tables. Back then, performers couldn't get work in any of the nightclubs unless they were connected to a mob guy, and the Riviera was a mecca for the mob. Gangsters from all over the country would go to the joint. They ran it."

The so-called mob connection to the Riviera and the secret gambling casino on the top floor added color to the fantastic canvas on which Bill Miller was painting his dream. Thanks to the newspaper reporters and columnists of the day, the Riviera became an ongoing soap opera that the public loved. What could be more exciting than to wine, dine and see a star-studded show at the Riviera and hopefully rub elbows with the baddest of the bad guys: mobsters who made the papers every day for the horrific lives they led. Every out-of-town businessman coming to New York wanted to be entertained at the Riviera and possibly be in the same room with the "goodfellas"

Show business has a funny way of reducing the most prominent people to mush when it comes to their meeting celebrities. In show business, it is not what actually is, it is what the public perceives it to be. In the instance of the Riviera, it was the perceived connection to the mob that partially made going there so entertaining, exciting and forbidden. It's interesting to think that the Riviera, a place that was so cheerful, well lit and completely safe, was perceived by the public to have a dark side.

Bill Miller played the dark side card to the limit. He would never affirm or deny that the Riviera was "connected." Miller never complained about the write-ups in the syndicated newspaper columns every day that reported on the comings and goings of the famous and infamous while they were at the Riviera.

Although most people are of the opinion that Bill Miller's partners were mob connected, it was unlikely. Miller's main partner in the Riviera was Sam Marcus, who had bought the Embassy Club from Miller some years before. Bill Miller and Sam Marcus had met years ago when Miller was a well-known nightclub owner and operator. Marcus was an active entrepreneur in many businesses and was principally engaged in the photographic supply field. In April 1946, they purchased additional property from Michael Realty Company, which was located in Fort Lee, New Jersey. The financing for the Riviera's purchase included a $300,000 purchase money mortgage held by Ben Marden, along with Marcus contributing $93,750, Al Bierman $20,000 and Robert Schwartz $11,250, making the purchase price $425,000 on the record. Bill Miller executed and delivered a $50,000 demand note, his portion of the financing, dated April 1, 1946, to Marcus. The name of the corporation they formed was Milmar, combining the names of Miller and Marcus. Milmar Corporation was the owner of the real estate.

A silent partner in the later deal was Al Kevelson. Miller had anticipated that it would be Kevelson who would eventually join up with him to handle the ultimate transaction to pay off Ben Marden. Al and his two brothers made their fortune owning and operating the Ace Asbestos Manufacturing Company in Jersey City. The logo for the company was an ace of spades, with the skyline of New York in the background.

The popular opinion of the public was that the Riviera had mob connections, and most likely that originated through word of mouth, passed on by the customers themselves telling exciting stories to their friends about their experiences during their night at the Riviera and being in the presence of the notorious gangsters who took up so much of the news print in the tabloids. During that period in American history, the gangsters were actually treated like celebrities. It's no wonder that so many people thought that the place had mob connections; so many notorious mobsters frequented the club on a routine basis that it would be easy to think that they owned it. This was in conjunction with the legendary secret gambling casino on the top floor that everyone seemed to know about. Miller, on the other hand, probably loved the idea of the mobsters in his audience because they were just another part of the Riviera experience that pleased and excited his clientele. The mob guys were celebrities, just like Mickey Mantle and Sugar Ray Robinson, and their mere presences created an electric atmosphere and a lot of quiet excitement.

Miller, understanding what pleased his customers, always insisted that his partners take an active interest in the business by mingling among the guests and being friendly. Miller never had any trouble meeting and greeting people—that was his forte—but the others were not made of the same fabric and found it difficult. Joey Bishop commented in an interview some years later that Bill Miller was the kind of guy who would allow a comedian to use him as the brunt of the joke and then just laugh it off. "He was a great boss, and everybody loved him," Bishop said.

SAVING THE PALISADES

B ill Miller never met John D. Rockefeller Jr., but their interests crossed at one point, and Rockefeller prevailed. That wasn't a surprise, since John D. was father of the five powerful Rockefeller brothers, grandsons of John D. Rockefeller Sr., who in his time was the wealthiest person in the world. The Rockefeller family—during the period when their business and philanthropic activities were headed by John D. Sr. and, later, John D. Jr.—controlled Standard Oil of New Jersey (later called Exxon), the Chase Manhattan Bank, Rockefeller Center and Rock Resorts and had interests in mining, communications and myriad other enterprises.

As important as the preservation of the Rockefeller fortune was to John D. Jr. and his sons, equally important was the Rockefeller legacy in carrying out meaningful philanthropy, which set the standard for philanthropic endeavors in the United States for all time. The family contributed vast sums of money to purchase the land for the establishment of Grand Teton, Yosemite and Acadia National Parks. Preserving Fort Washington in northwest Manhattan and turning it into a city park was a Rockefeller project, as was the establishment of the Cloisters, a medieval art museum at the base of Fort Washington. The Rockefellers funded the development of Memorial Sloan-Kettering Cancer Center; Rockefeller University for Medical Science; Spelman College in Atlanta, Georgia; the University of Chicago; Colonial Williamsburg; and the Museum of Modern Art. Nelson Rockefeller, the future governor of New York and vice president of the United States, purchased seventeen acres on Manhattan's East Side and gave them to the United Nations for its headquarters complex.

Is that all there is? *Courtesy of the Palisades Interstate Park Commission.*

While there are literally hundreds of Rockefeller-funded projects in the United States and abroad, only one had an impact on Bill Miller and the Riviera. Since the 1800s, individuals and organizations fought to preserve the majestic Palisades that run along the western side of the Hudson River from Jersey City, New Jersey, to Piermont, New York, a distance of twenty miles. Quarrying of the solid rock formation that overlooked the Hudson River for millions of years was a major enterprise from the middle of the nineteenth century until 1900, when the destruction was abruptly stopped. The New Jersey Women's Federation fought mightily to save the Palisades from further damage, and on December 24, 1899, the quarrying stopped. The Carpenters Brothers' quarry was the worst offender, and just before the ban was made public, the brothers blew up hundreds of tons of the historic cliffs to produce small rocks for road construction fill. They, like many others from that period, had absolutely no interest in the preservation of the prehistoric cliff range, which isn't duplicated anywhere else.

Rockefeller Sr. had made a modest contribution to a project headed by Mary Harriman, wife of E.H. Harriman, president of the Union Pacific Railroad. The Harrimans contributed ten thousand acres of land and $1 million to the formation of the Highlands of the Hudson Forest Preserve that eventually became the Harriman–Bear Mountain State Park, which later became a part of the Palisades Interstate Park. Some forty years later, John D. Jr. found himself enchanted with the Palisades and devoted a great deal of time, effort and money to returning the great rock formation to its natural state, a time when only the Lenape Indians occupied the forests along its top.

Across the Hudson River at the northern end of the Palisades, on the highest point in Westchester County, New York, is Pocantico Hills, the home of the legendary Rockefeller family. The 3,500-acre property was purchased by John D. Rockefeller Sr. in 1893, and the estate was completed in 1913. The property's centerpiece is Kykuit Manor, a forty-room fieldstone Georgian Revival structure that would fit into the suburban neighborhoods of Paris. Kykuit Manor was tastefully furnished, and a balcony on the fourth floor offered brilliant views of the Hudson River and the Palisades.

When Kykuit Manor was designed, John D. Sr. was careful not to emulate his brother William's estate, Rockwood Hall, which boasted 204 rooms. Rockwood Hall was built directly above the Hudson River about two miles from Kykuit on the site of a former colonial brickyard that had supplied the red bricks for the early structures along the river. William Rockefeller purchased the two-hundred-acre property, which contained a castle that was an example of a popular building style in the Hudson Valley in the nineteenth century. No one is certain about whether Rockefeller razed the castle or enlarged it. After William's death in 1922, the property was largely ignored, and in 1942, John D. Sr. had Rockwood Hall demolished and the debris dumped into the Hudson River.

William Rockefeller had enjoyed the Washington Irving short story "The Legend of Sleepy Hollow," which purports to take place along the old Albany Post Road that ran parallel to the river. William paid for the replacement of the Headless Horseman Bridge featured in Irving's story, as well as for the preservation of the Old Dutch Church and Sleepy Hollow Cemetery, which are popular stops on Washington Irving literary tours.

John D. Rockefeller Sr. passed away in 1937, and John D. Jr. took firm hold of the family's future. He continued his father's business and philanthropic activities and raised his five sons to become leaders in American society. The Pocantico Hills compound was its own compact society. Eventually, seventy-five buildings, about half of them homes, were added. The Rockefellers maintained a herd of Black Angus cattle for their consumption and sold off some at a profit. The estate had a medical staff, and a public school was constructed just outside the main gate. Their farms produced enough vegetables for the family and staff, but seafood was purchased at the Gristedes Brothers market on Broadway in Tarrytown. The Rockefellers were hardly recluses, and they took to public life with vigor.

John D. Jr. would gaze out from his fourth-floor balcony admiring the commercial shipping traffic on the Hudson River. He had an unobstructed view of the Palisades from the George Washington Bridge north to their termination in Piermont, New York. His enjoyment was limited, however, because he could see the great mansions built along the top of the steep cliffs, the most offensive sight of all being a place known as Bill Miller's Riviera. Its giant electric sign and yellow-and-blue exterior clearly didn't belong in Rockefeller's world and certainly not on the top of a great natural wonder.

Developing the Palisades Interstate Park project was supported by the Harriman family of New York. The Harrimans were another extremely wealthy family known for public service and philanthropy. The Harrimans had contributed part of their forty-thousand-acre estate for the creation of Harriman State Park. Later, Harriman-owned land was the majority of the acres that made up Harriman, Bear Mountain, Sterling Forest and Palisades State Parks, for an astounding total of seventy thousand acres. John D. Jr., of course, knew the Harrimans and agreed to assist in the preservation of the Palisades and in the creation of an interstate park.

Rockefeller began to buy up properties that dotted the landscape from Englewood Cliffs north. It was agreed that property south of the Washington Bridge was too densely populated and could not be recovered. However, homes and businesses along the riverbank at the foot of the Palisades were purchased as well, and most were razed, except for some historic buildings. Rio Vista, the estate of Manuel Rionda, was leveled, as was Cliff Dale, George Zabriski's estate, the largest house on the Palisades. Rionda, originally from Spain, owned sugar plantations in Cuba. The Zabriski name can be traced, in Bergen County, back one hundred years before the American Revolution. Rockefeller had insisted that the skyline of the Palisades be preserved, so the mansions fell. The Cora Timken estate, where Timken's husband, Dr. John Burnett, experimented with the healing properties of electromagnetism, was also leveled, but the serpentine-shaped swimming pool was spared and can still be seen by hikers. The John Ringling mansion, Gray Crag, was also demolished. The Ringling family of the circus world moved to Sarasota, Florida, taking the treasures they had collected from all over the world, which can be viewed in their former Venetian-style mansion, now the Ringling Museum, which is operated by the State of Florida. In 1925, John Ringling was one of the world's richest men, but he couldn't preserve his property on the Palisades.

The Palisades were saved from commercial exploitation by Rockefeller and the Park Commission. A few parts of the old estates still exist, but they are nearly covered by thick vines and shrubs that grow unchecked in the park. There are foundations, chimneys and fountains, and it has been said that the outline of the Palisades Mountain House, an epic hotel that accommodated five hundred guests, can be found in Englewood Cliffs. Parts of the Palisades remain mysterious. Few records were kept regarding the estates and their owners. Condemnation proceedings, as well as private purchases, went on for twenty years, with Bill Miller's Riviera succumbing in 1953.

1953

THE YEAR THE
RIVIERA CLOSED

In 1953, the ill winds of change came and worked their way along the cliffs of the Palisades, arriving on the scene and blowing away just about every trace of what once was one of the greatest nightclubs. The Riviera's physical presence was gone, but snippets of the legacy it left can be still seen on every major nightclub and showroom stage around the world.

Change is always inevitable; sometimes it is welcome, and sometimes it is not. But no matter which side your luck falls on, it is best to put your chips down on the certainty that change will surely take place. The year 1953 ushered in a new president of the United States, Dwight D. Eisenhower, inaugurated as the thirty-fourth president. He succeeded Harry S Truman, who left Washington inauguration evening with his wife, Bess, on an ordinary train that took them to Independence, Missouri. Television coverage of Eisenhower's inauguration was sent to 21 million TV sets in homes across the country. In 1919, when Jean Richard bought the Villa Richard, radio broadcasting was almost nonexistent. Newspapers were the medium that people relied on to disseminate the information of the day. In 1953, the world was changing fast.

General Motors introduced the first American sports car that year; the two-seater was called a Corvette, and it was displayed at the Motorama show at the Waldorf-Astoria. The Corvette's most unique feature was its fiberglass body. The car was available in limited quantities after June 1953, and every one was presold.

The rest of the world wasn't quite as peaceful in 1953. President Eisenhower announced that he would pull the Seventh Fleet out of the

Formosa Straits to permit the nationalist Chinese to attack communist China. Also, in Russia, leaders of the alleged Jewish "Doctors Plot" were arrested. They were accused of conspiring to murder the Soviet leadership.

Of course, not everything took on such serious consequences. J. Fred Muggs, a chimpanzee, became a regular on NBC's *Today Show*. *Peter Pan*, a film made by Walt Disney, opened at the Roxy Theater in New York. The Roxy was as large as the Radio City Music Hall and had its own version of the Rockette dancers who performed with a full orchestra and vocalists with the showing of every movie. The *Adventures of Superman* TV series premiered in syndication.

One of the biggest news stories of the day was the treason case against Ethel and Julius Rosenberg, a married couple involved in a plot to give the secret plans for the manufacture of the atomic bomb to the Soviet Union. President Eisenhower refused to give the Rosenbergs clemency, while Pope Pius XII was asking the United States to grant mercy to the convicted spies.

The Rosenbergs were convicted of passing secrets to the Soviet Union and were sentenced to death. Supreme Court justice William O. Douglas stayed the executions of the spies, which was scheduled for June 18, to allow them to celebrate their fourteenth wedding anniversary, only to have their execution carried out the following day at Sing Sing prison in Ossining, New York. The Rosenbergs were prosecuted by assistant United States attorney Roy Cohn, a protégé of the infamous red baiter and confirmed liar Senator Joe McCarthy of Wisconsin. Cohn knew that his vigorous prosecution, even though the evidence was slim and the government was overreacting, would give him lifetime credentials with the politically extreme right element in the country.

In February 1953, United States Force F-84 Thunder jets raided a North Korean base on the Yalu River, the border between North Korea and China. In an unrelated incident, baseball's superstar Ted Williams was uninjured when his plane was shot down in Korea. Williams, a captain in the Marine Corps, was a fighter pilot in World War II and the Korean War.

One of the best movies of 1953 was William Inge's *Picnic*, starring William Holden and Kim Novak. Probably one of the greatest romantic scenes ever shot for the silver screen was when Holden and Novak were at the picnic. As the day was ending, the song "Moonglow" was playing in the background, and they saw each other while Kim was just moving to the music alone on the picnic grounds patio. They faced each other and began clapping their hands from afar to the rhythm of the music. They approached each other, slowly stepping in time to the music and clapping their hands, their eyes locked together. The scene was fantastic to those who enjoy romantic interludes.

The military back in 1953 was not immune from committing huge blunders. On March 11, a U.S. Air Force B-47 accidentally dropped a nuclear bomb on South Carolina; of course, the bomb did not go off because the fail-safe combinations had not been activated.

Speaking of bombs dropping, a huge one was dropped when the Boston Braves baseball team announced that the team was moving to Milwaukee that year and another when it was announced that Bill Miller's Riviera was condemned and was being razed to make way for the Palisades Interstate Parkway.

A wonderful announcement, on the other hand, was made when Dr. Jonas Salk, of the University of Pittsburgh announced that a vaccine against polio had been successfully tested by a small group of adults and children. By April 1955, the vaccine had undergone further testing and gained federal approval for public use. Salk's polio vaccine was so successful that by 1961 the cases of polio had decreased by 95 percent. It was discovered almost forty years later that the polio virus was chiefly transmitted by fecal contamination.

Walter Annenberg of Philadelphia published his first issue of *TV Guide*, and the first cover on that magazine featured a picture of Desi Arnaz, husband of television's most recognized star, Lucille Ball. Arnaz happened to be a contemporary and friend of the Riviera's Pupi Campo.

Executive Order No. 10450, signed by President Dwight D. Eisenhower, regarded security requirements for government employment. The order listed "sexual perversion" as a condition for firing a federal employee and for denying employment to potential applicants for federal jobs. Homosexuality, moral perversion and communism were categorized as national security threats. The issue of homosexual federal workers had become a dire federal personnel policy concern.

The Pulitzer Prize was awarded to Ernest Hemingway for his novella *The Old Man and the Sea*, and *Can Can* opened at the Shubert Theater on Broadway, to run for 892 performances.

Queen Elizabeth II of England was crowned in 1953 in Westminster Abbey. She began her reign as Queen of England sixteen months after her father, King George VI, passed away, and after her uncle, the Duke of Windsor, a Nazi sympathizer, abdicated the throne because of a romance with an American divorcée with a scandalous past.

In response to Republican senator Joseph McCarthy's tactics against alleged communists and un-American activities, Republican president

Eisenhower spoke out against "book burners" in June 1953 and "demagogues thirsty for personal power and public notice" in May 1954. Eisenhower also asserted the right of everybody to meet his accuser face to face. Eisenhower criticized McCarthy for opining that communists were even to be found in the Republican Party. However, it took McCarthy's accusatory attack on the U.S. Army to unseat him. Called before McCarthy's Senate committee, the army was accused of being riddled with communists and homosexuals. The army's lawyer, Joseph Welch, belittled McCarthy and exposed him as a liar and a fool. The McCarthy committee's chief counsel, Roy Cohn, thundered on about the security risk posed by homosexuals in the military, which was finally laid to rest in 2011. Roy Cohn died from complications of HIV/AIDS in 1986.

Later in October 1953, influential journalist Edward R. Murrow, on his TV show *See It Now*, brought to the attention of the public the abuses of power during the McCarthy era through his anticommunist campaign. Milo Radulovich, a U.S. Air Force Reserve officer, had been stripped of his commission for refusing to denounce his family, who subscribed to several Serbian newspapers. Radulovich's commission was later restored when Murrow took up his case and took the lead to discredit McCarthyism.

On July 26, 1953, a band of Cuban insurgents led by Fidel Castro revolted against President Fulgencio Batista, Cuba's latest dictator, with an unsuccessful attack on the Moncada army barracks in eastern Cuba. Castro was eventually captured and imprisoned on the Isle of Pines for the attack. In October, Castro was sentenced to fifteen years in prison. Six years later, Castro and his rebel army came out of the mountains, capturing Havana and successfully ousting Batista. Was Ben Marden's uncanny perception, years before, about the potentially unstable political atmosphere in Cuba the possible motivation that led him to make his decision to sell the Riviera and retire from the nightclub and casino business? One can only speculate that this might have been the case.

An armistice ending the fighting of the Korean War occurred on July 27, 1953. The representatives of the United Nations, Korea and China signed the papers in Panmunjom. Lieutenant General William K. Harrison represented the UN, and General Nam II represented North Korea. General Mark Clark, commander of the UN forces, added his signature to the armistice agreement. Thirty-three thousand Americans had died in the conflict, and eight thousand were still missing as late as the year 2000.

Times were really changing for the airlines that year, with Eastern Airlines entering the jet age with the Electra propjet. The advent of passenger jet travel opened up the Caribbean, South America and, later, the rest of the world to vacationers. Las Vegas became a four-hour destination from anywhere in the nation.

Les Paul and Mary Ford recorded their number one seller "Vaya con Dios" using Les's fantastic new innovation of stacking the tape machine, allowing Mary to overdub her voice and sing her own harmonies. Les and Mary lived at the time in Mahwah, New Jersey.

Speaking of inventions, that year NBC experimented with using a color broadcast of the show *Kukla, Fran and Ollie*, a Burr Tillstrom original creation. It was a blast for the public to see that broadcast, providing that their sets could pick up the colors.

Another blast that took place was the announcement that the Soviet Union had successfully tested a hydrogen bomb, an act that set fear into the hearts of all in the free world.

Red Barber resigned as the Dodgers' sportscaster to join the Yankees, and Mickey Mantle hit a home run in Washington's Griffith Stadium off the Senators' Chuck Stobbs that was entered into the *Guinness Book of World Records* as measuring 565 feet. In addition to those items, the Supreme Court upheld a 1922 ruling that Major League Baseball did not come within the scope of federal antitrust laws.

Senator John F. Kennedy and Jacqueline Bouvier married in Newport, Rhode Island.

After a successful run at Bill Miller's Riviera, followed by an appearance on the Ed Sullivan show, musical humorist Victor Borge opened his "Comedy in Music" show at the Golden Theater on Broadway. It ran for 849 performances.

Pakistan became an Islamic republic in November.

The Riviera was not the only thing getting ready to close that year. The long-running show *Guys and Dolls*, based on the stories of Damon Runyon, closed at the Forty-sixth Street Theater after 1,200 performances. It's ironic that the show whose characters emulated those that might be found at the Riviera was also closing. In its place, the show *Kismet* opened on Broadway at the Ziegfeld Theater and ran for 583 performances.

Hugh Hefner, setting out to shake up society, published the first issue of *Playboy* magazine in December 1953. On the cover was Marilyn Monroe, and she was the first nude *Playboy* centerfold. This was a monumental act because it defied so many laws, but Hefner won all of the lawsuits against him and changed what adults can see, read and hear forever.

The Riviera was on a downward slide. Its time was passing. By the time 1953 rolled around, the computer had been invented, jet propulsion was commonplace, color television was in its infancy, polio had been conquered, Kinsey had published *Sexual Behavior in the Human Female* (the first major survey on women's sexual habits), Ian Fleming had published his first James Bond book (*Casino Royal*), *Playboy* magazine had taken the country by storm and Dizzy Gillespie had bent his trumpet bell upward at Snookie's in Manhattan. Younger customers came to clubs and wanted different music and new musical personalities. The sexual revolution, the women's movement and civil rights ran headfirst into the anti–Vietnam War protests of the 1960s.

Music was beginning to change in 1953. The big bands were on their way out, replaced by vocal groups and combos like the Platters, a group made up of Joe Jefferson, Cornell Gunther, Alex Hodge and Herb Reed on vocals, as well as a female singer named Zola. During one of the last Riviera shows, Eddie Fisher sang his new hit record, "Oh My Pa-Pa (To Me He Was So Wonderful)." In 1953, Eddie's song made it to the top of the charts. The Riviera was losing its cachet. Its patrons were retiring and moving south. The colorful criminal element was under attack and would be defeated over the next two decades. Entertainment was available free at home through ever expanding television productions. Even the motion picture studios were worried until the advent of videotape, and then the studios became production houses for television shows.

Although the song of Bill Miller's Riviera has ended, its memory still lingers on.

ENCORE

B en Marden joined the U.S. Navy at the outbreak of World War I. Upon his discharge after the war, not much is known about Ben's personal life other than his rapid rise to the top of an entertainment empire that started with his ownership, along with some silent partners, of the Colonial Inn in Hallandale, Florida. The gambling casino in that venue set the stage for Ben's future affiliations throughout his career. From there, Ben went on to own the world-famous Cotton Club in Manhattan's Harlem. In addition, he opened the Palais Royal, an upscale showroom in midtown Manhattan, making a success of that as well.

Ben was known as a man who had an eye for the ladies. In 1944, he met socialite Alma Slocum Dupuy, with whom he carried on a lengthy relationship. After Ben's death, Alma claimed that they had entered into a common-law marriage and that she was entitled to inherit an interest in his sizable estate. When the matter was brought to trial, twenty-one days of testimony were heard. During the testimony, Ben was described as being an aggressive and domineering type of man, but he had a very charming side, too. He was also described as "an inveterate philanderer" based on the string of ladies he courted. It was stated during testimony that he lavished them with gifts and also remembered them in his will. It was also noted that his enduring affection was for his second wife, with whom he had children.

While his ventures in nightclubs in Florida and New York were going on, Ben was told that the George Washington Bridge was going to be built between Fort Lee, New Jersey, and upper Manhattan. Ben jumped at the opportunity and bought the Villa Richard, only to watch it burn down a few years later, which made way for his next giant venture: the construction of the new Riviera in Fort Lee.

The Riviera was open from April to October, so Ben could take his handpicked staff of waiters, captains and cooks to Cuba to cater to his guests at the Hotel Nacional in Havana, where he was the manager, at least on the surface. After the Riviera was sold to Bill Miller, Ben, using his years of experience in Cuba and the contacts he had gathered, arranged the purchase of Cuba's Cadena Axul radio network from Amado Trinidad for $1 million in 1946. It was stressed in a United States Foreign Service dispatch that there was a lot of resentment among the Cuban broadcasters who were afraid that American investors might seize control of all Cuban radio and television stations. There was a lack of trust by Cubans regarding the motives of Americans and the United States government in particular. This attitude was the result of America's ignoring Spain's death grip on Cuba until 1898.

When Fulgencio Batista assumed power, Gaspar Pumarejo, a businessman, saw a chance to earn a commission on the sale of the network, and with this mind, he approached the new Cuban dictator for his backing. About that time, Edmund A. Chester, of the Columbia Broadcasting System, went to Havana to interview his old friend Batista for CBS. Apparently, the purchase of the radio network was discussed, and for about a month, Pumarejo and Chester worked together on the proposed sale, which was to be financed by Ben Marden, with President Batista receiving a percentage.

Chester and Pumarejo quarreled, however, over who was to be president of the network, and the latter withdrew from the project. With Ben Marden's financial backing, Edmund Chester purchased all of the shares of RHC. Batista remained dictator of Cuba for twenty-five years and turned the island into the "Latin Las Vegas," a playground for Americans, controlled by Meyer Lansky on behalf of the American mafia. American government policy toward Cuba was controlled by politicians in Washington who had close ties to the members of the national crime syndicate or to Meyer Lansky directly. No one could predict how influential Cuba would become in America's affairs. After Fidel Castro overthrew the Batista dictatorship and installed himself as president, relations between the United States and Cuba rapidly deteriorated.

A persistent theory that claims to identify the people who were behind the assassination of President John F. Kennedy suggests that a combination of anti-Castro Cubans, the mafia and American intelligence agents who worked with both groups carried out the murder in retaliation for the failed support of the Bay of Pigs invasion that was supposed to unseat Castro. The Cubans, of course, wanted to return to their homeland; members of the mafia wanted to reopen the casinos, which eventually they were able to do; and the intelligence community believed that Kennedy was "soft on communism." Ben Marden, of course, didn't know that his activities in Cuba in the 1950s, his friendship with Batista or his business relationship with Meyer Lansky would have even the slightest influence on the course of American history. Cuba remains a contentious political issue in the United States, with third-generation Cuban Americans demanding an answer to the fifty-year-old question: what is the future of Cuba?

Ben Marden wasn't all business. He had a soft spot for people less fortunate than himself. He proved this time and time again, beginning with the policy of preparing at least five hundred food baskets every Thanksgiving for needy families. He also donated heavily to charities like Parents Anonymous, which took care of needy children. In addition, he was a major contributor to programs for children with developmental disabilities long before the broad spectrum of these issues was identified.

Marden was really a man of great mystery. While he was in the public eye due to the nightclubs he owned, his personal life and his affiliations with persons like Meyer Lansky were not known even by his business associates. Marden was never accused of any illegal activities, even though he participated in the ownership of restaurants and nightclubs where gambling took place. In Ben's world, however, gambling was considered a harmless vice, and he managed to stay above the really illegal activities that were carried out by those who operated the casinos.

Ben lived on West Fifty-fifth Street in Manhattan in an apartment building that he owned. He was an unusually generous landlord. He had air conditioning units installed in the apartments occupied by elderly tenants at no charge, and he had a policy of never issuing an eviction notice to any tenants who were down on their luck and behind on their rent. After years of running restaurants, nightclubs, casinos and associating with legendary show business stars, public officials on all levels and infamous gangsters—Ben lived quietly during his last years. He passed away at age seventy-seven.

In 1953, the Riviera closed and Bill Miller found himself without a place to go every day. He felt obligated to do everything he could to ensure that his acts found new venues in which to perform. The major headliners, of course, were not affected, but the supporting acts had depended on appearances at the Riviera at top pay. Bill, uncertain if he would ever own and operate a top-flight nightclub again, was reduced to sitting back and watching Jack Entratta, a former Copacabana partner, sign many of Miller's acts to contracts to appear at the new Sands Hotel in Las Vegas. The musical, dance and comedy talent that Miller so painstakingly put together over many years was being lost to Entratta and the Sands. The one consolation was that Miller had a great amount of money awarded to him from the eminent domain proceedings when the Palisades Interstate Park Commission took the Riviera's property to clear the way for an entrance to the George Washington Bridge and an extension of the parkway to Fort Lee.

No sooner did the wrecking ball hit Miller's beloved Riviera than a call came in from Milton Prell, who had always had respect for Bill and his ability to bring out the best in the performers he represented. Prell had opened the new Sahara Hotel in Las Vegas, which would be in competition with the Sands, as well as the other hotels on the Vegas Strip.

Prell offered Miller the opportunity to purchase a 10 percent share of the Sahara's stock and to be the become hotel's entertainment director. Miller accepted the proposal but was faced with the serious dilemma of how to field a new slate of acts made up of great people he had become friends with over the years. In reality, those people and their acts were not the top-level performers Miller had used to fill his bill at the Riviera. Some of Miller's new prospects didn't even have a nightclub act at all. Miller was starting all over again from the beginning, and his pride and reputation were at stake; the odds of making it in Las Vegas, among all of the competition, didn't look very promising.

Starting over wasn't new to Miller, and the first act he hired for the Sahara was Ray Bolger, the scarecrow from the 1939 MGM motion picture *The Wizard of Oz*. Bolger had the one important ingredient, aside from being good at acting like a scarecrow, that Miller liked: he was a great dancer. Bolger could dance up a storm. "When in doubt, hire a dancer," Miller would always quip. Bill met with Ray Bolger and convinced him that, deep down under all that scarecrow stuff, there was a great nightclub act waiting to come out, and under Miller's guidance, Bolger's best performance would emerge. Bill Miller knew that up to now no one had taken advantage of what Ray Bolger had to offer. Miller decided that if Bolger was showcased as a master of ceremonies, and did his dance routine between announcing the acts, the audience would love it. They did. And Bolger and Miller opened with great reviews.

Donald O'Connor, another dancer who was also great in films and dance revues, was the next to work for Miller. Once again, Coach Miller called the right play, and Donald hit the field and was racking up the score. Miller was on a roll now. Bill's confidence began to grow once again, and he was beginning to breathe a little easier in Las Vegas. He felt that mysterious women always attracted attention, and no one had more feminine mystique than movie star Marlene Dietrich. He correctly figured that her sensual presence on stage was more important than her act. He was right. Marlene packed the showroom at the Sahara. Marlene's musical director was Burt Bacharach.

Reportedly, Dietrich was paid $30,000 per week by the Sahara, and she was worth it. Wearing her famous "nude dress," she filled the main room night after night. Marlene had worked tirelessly during World War II to entertain American troops near the front lines in Algeria, Italy, England and France, and she accompanied General Patton on his army's drive through Germany. Marlene was born in Berlin in 1901 but hated Hitler and his Nazi party. She became an American citizen in 1937. The United States government awarded Marlene Dietrich the Medal of Freedom, the highest civilian award, for her efforts to improve the morale of servicemen in the field.

The war veterans remembered Dietrich and her appearances in their war-torn places. They found her show at the Sahara and came to see her—the woman who had been there for them. After her last show each night, Marlene would spend time with the veterans, especially the ones who were disabled. Often she stayed in a hotel bar all night talking and singing with them.

Miller's team, consisting of Ray Bolger, Donald O'Connor and Marlene Dietrich, was competing against the future members of the "Rat Pack," consisting of headliners who had gotten their starts at the Riviera. Frank Sinatra, Dean Martin, Sammy Davis Jr. and Joey Bishop were all hugely successful at the Sands, and Las Vegas insiders predicted that Miller and his current stable of untested nightclub acts would disappear without a trace. That, however, didn't happen because once again Miller's genius showed through like a beacon in the desert.

Miller was using up his limited collection of talent, and he was at the crossroads trying to decide what to do next when the Sicilian-American gravel-voiced supertalent named Louis Prima surfaced. Miller had represented Prima some years before, booking him into a small New York club in 1944 called the Famous Door, located on Fifty-second Street. The New Orleans phenomenon, as Prima was known, took New York by storm and set the trend for Italian music. It was Prima who coined the terms "swing" and "hep" and the phrase "Crazy, man." His recordings of Italian songs like "Angelina," "Josephina," "Please Don't Ringa the Bell" and "Bachigaloop" were only the first in the series of his lifelong string of hits that included "Old Black Magic," "When You're Smilin," "Bona Sera" and "Robin Hood." Louis Prima also wrote the song that crowned Benny Goodman as the "King of Swing": "Sing, Sing, Sing," featuring Gene Krupa on the drums. Louis also cowrote the wonderful ballad called "A Sunday Kind of Love." Prima's compositions performed by other vocalists sold millions of records, making him one of the most important composers of popular music in the mid-twentieth century. Unlike the current system of compensation for musical artists, composers and vocalists in the past saw little earning from their record deals. By all rights, Louis Prima should have been a rich man; instead, he was hoping to get back on the top of the music business by appearing in Las Vegas.

Coauthor Ron Kase with parents Johannah and Gustave Kase in Havana, Cuba, in 1948. Gustave had interests in cigar manufacturing. *Courtesy of the Kase family collection.*

Bill Miller also remembered that Louis Prima and his twenty-two-piece band had packed New York's Paramount Theater on three separate occasions in one year, a record that was never broken. But all of that was back in the late 1940s. Could Louis do it again? Bill bet that he could.

Bill Miller, understanding the caliber of Louis' talent, was happy to take the chance and book him at the Sahara, but the main showroom was booked with talent for almost a year in advance, so the great Louis Prima was booked as a lounge act. Here were two great talents whose better days, up to now, were behind them. However, both were willing to take the gamble and go for it one more time. Louis Prima arrived in Las Vegas happy to have gotten Miller's summons. He drove from New Orleans in his orange-and-white

1953 Oldsmobile 98 Fiesta convertible, one of General Motors' "futuristic cars." The Fiesta was offered by GM for only one season, and only 458 were produced. Prima loved his Fiesta and was proud that he owned one of the scarce automobiles, for which he paid $5,717 in cash (equivalent to $46,000 today). Prima looked good, dressed well and drove a newly classic car, but he needed to get back in the show business game.

Louis remembering that it was Bill Miller who booked him when he needed the work most and was also in Las Vegas to pay back the debt. When the two met, Louis explained that the days of the big bands were nearing their end and that he had put together a small aggregation of the best handpicked musicians in the business. He said that his brother, Leon, found him a sax player in New Orleans named Sam Butera who, according to Louis, was the best tenor sax player in the world. He went on to explain that his new group was called the Witnesses, and it was made up of Jack Marshall on guitar, Willie McCumber Jr. on keyboard, Bobby Morris on drums and Armando Rodriques on bass. He also said that a new singer named Keely Smith was appearing with him. She was of American Indian heritage and could sing her brains out. Prima, who up to now had always been exclusively featured in the main room of every venue he ever played, was now asked by the genius Miller if he would consider stepping down a notch and accept performing with the band in the Casbah Lounge at the Sahara.

"The lounge? How could you ask me to play the lounge?" asked Louis. Miller told him that if he agreed to play the lounge, he would sign him to a seven-year contract and that he and his group would be paid more money than they had ever dreamed of making. Miller was so sure that his plan would work that he offered them $10,500 per week to start, which is equivalent to earning $84,000 in 2010, a really nice paycheck. Louis and Bill shook hands on the deal, and the result of that agreement was reported in the *Las Vegas Review Journal*: "No one in the history of show business did the business that Louis Prima did from midnight to six in the morning." It was one of the biggest things to happen in Las Vegas.

In retrospect, Miller figured that if he had the best after-hours show on the Vegas Strip, the world would beat a path to his door, and that they did, year after year. When all of the other shows finished their late-night performances on the Vegas Strip, the patrons, musicians, stars and celebrities in town to see those shows would all show up at the Casbah Lounge for a nightcap and catch Louis, Keeley and Sam and the Witnesses. No one slept when Louis was holding court in the Casbah Lounge.

Bill Miller's success in Las Vegas continued. In 1955, he left the Sahara, bought an interest in the Dunes and teamed up with his old friend and producer Donn Arden to put on some fantastic "feather" shows: the Follies Bergere and Lido de Paris. In April 1956, Miller went over to the New Frontier Hotel and caught a show where some new kid from Memphis was appearing with his three-piece group made up of Scotty Moore, Bill Black and D.J. Fontana. Everything was all wrong, according to the way Bill Miller saw things. The Frontier had booked the country group on the same bill as Freddy Martin, a band leader whose days had long passed, with his hits in the late 1930s and early 1940s. For example, Freddy Martin's big tune in 1941 was Tchaikovsky's B-flat piano concerto called "Tonight We Love." The critics panned the group. Bill Willard, a reviewer for the *Las Vegas Sun* newspaper, crucified the performance, writing, "For teenagers the long tall Memphis lad is a whiz; for the average Vegas spender or show goer, he is a bore. His musical sound with a combo of three is uncouth, matching to a great extent the lyric content of his nonsensical songs." Bill Miller, in the audience that night at the Frontier, saw something entirely different. He felt that this young man, Elvis Presley, was neither a country western singer nor a rock-and-roller; he was something brand new and was surely going to be one of the most important performers of all time.

After the show, Bill went backstage and invited Elvis and his band over to the Casbah Lounge at the Sahara for a drink. Elvis and the band accepted because between shows they would always bounce around the towns they played and would frequent the lounges anyway, so when Miller made the offer, they went willingly.

Performing in the Casbah Lounge at the Sahara Hotel that night was a group called Freddie Bell and the Bell Boys. Freddie and his group had a small hit back in 1955 called "Hound Dog." Elvis and the boys liked it so much that they decided to record it the next time they went to the studio, and of course it became one of Elvis's greatest hits. Elvis, at the time, was under contract to the Frontier, so Miller couldn't hire him on the spot. But later, Bill Miller did manage to book him into the International Hotel, and the "King" went on to become a performer like no other.

After one of the most illustrious careers in show business, Bill Miller quietly retired to Palm Springs in the mid-1970s. Show business lost a great one when he passed away in December 2002 at the age of ninety-eight. His legacy as the creator of America's Showplace should have a tag on it that says, "Built by one of America's greatest and kindest showmen."

The Riviera's closing in 1953 began to sound the death knell for the era of roadhouses, nightclubs and ballrooms around the United States. One of the main reasons for this happening was that James Petrillo—who became the president of Musicians Local 10 out of Chicago and ultimately led the American Federation of Musicians from 1940 to 1958—made a career out of organizing musicians. Petrillo's efforts ensured that musicians earned living wages but in turn put tremendous pressure on the owners of the marginally successful establishments that employed musicians. Not every club, roadhouse or ballroom was doing the business that clubs like the Riviera and Copacabana were doing, and Petrillo's demands financially suffocated the small establishments, forcing them to either go out of business or hire fewer musicians.

It was the hiring of fewer musicians that led to the practice of putting together combinations of instruments that were compatible with one another. Louis Prima's transition from his big band to his combo called the Witnesses was also a result of the economics of the times.

As the combos gained in proficiency and popularity beginning in the early 1950s and developed throughout the decade, successful combos with names like Bill Haley and the Comets and Buddy Holley and the Crickets came into being, and even Elvis performed with a combo. The ballrooms that once resounded with the sounds of sixteen-piece bands now rocked with four or five musicians aided with huge speakers and newly invented Les Paul electric guitars.

Mobster Bugsy Siegel's insights in converting the desert to an oasis, supported by Meyer Lansky's brilliant organizational skills, also contributed to the demise of the roadhouses, ballrooms and supper clubs. When Las Vegas opened up with hotel accommodations and showrooms together, no longer was it necessary for patrons to drive home after seeing a show or sneak into a secret room to play a little blackjack. The patrons could openly and legally enjoy gambling before and after seeing the dazzling shows and then retire to their luxurious suite without worrying about who was to be the designated driver. The Riviera and places like it paved the way for today's great hotels and casinos in Las Vegas, Atlantic City, Foxwoods and the lesser places springing up around the nation. None, however, had the cachet and mystique of Bill Miller's Riviera, a place like no other, a place that represented an entire era before the Internet, before smartphones, Facebook and the concept of immediate social networking was available to everyone.

When you visit Fort Lee, New Jersey, try to join a trail walk offered by the Palisades Interstate Park Commission along the Palisades that stops among the ruins of Bill Miller's Riviera. If one stands perfectly still near the cliff's edge and listens to the wind, he might hear the refrain:

It seems we stood and talked like this before…

BIBLIOGRAPHY

Beitler, Stu. "Fort Lee, NJ Nightclub Fire, Nov 1936." GenDisasters: Events that Touched Our Ancestors' Lives. http://www3.gendisasters.com/new-york/10761/fort-lee-nj-nightclub-fire-nov-1936.

Biographical Directory of the United States Congress. "Kefauver, Carey Estes." http://bioguide.congress.gov/scripts/biodisplay.pl?index=k000044.

Champion, Marge, dancer at the Riviera with husband Gower Champion. Personal interview with authors, April 21, 2011.

Deed between Michael Realty Company and William Miller and Samuel Marcus of the City, County and State of NY. Deed Book No. 2622, page 213, #16881. Concerns the purchase of additional land for the Riviera.

Evans, K.J. "Bill Miller: Mr. Entertainment." The First 100, part 2, Resort Rising. *Las Vegas Review Journal*. www.1st100.com/part2/miller.html.

Gilvey, John Anthony. *Before the Parade Passes By: Gower Champion and the Glorious American Musical*. New York: St. Martin's Press, 2005.

Harrell, Raymond L., Attaché. "RHC Radio Network Sold to American Interests." Foreign Service Dispatch. American Embassy Dispatch No. 1410, Havana, February 29, 1952.

Harris, Drew, Associate Judge. Court of Appeal of Florida, Third District. *Estate Ben Marden v. Gertrude Bacon*, January 24, 1978. http://fl.findacase. com/research/wfrmDocViewer.aspx/xq/fac.19780124_0040567. fl.htm/qx.

Havana Post. "Ed Chester Comes Back Home." April 22, 1952.

Kelley, Tina. "Bill Miller, 98, Impresario in the Golden Age." *New York Times*, December 12, 2002.

Klara, Robert. "Riviera of Dreams" "Exit Ramp" column. *New Jersey Monthly*, 1995.

Lacey, Robert. *Meyer Lansky and the Gangster Life*. Boston: Little, Brown and Company, 1991.

McLellan, Dennis. "Bill Miller, 98, Vegas Hotels Entertainment Director, Club Owner." *Los Angeles Times*, December 25, 2002.

Miami Herald. Abe Vine's Obituary. June 2, 2011.

Nevada Observer. "Investigation of Organized Crime in Interstate Commerce Friday July 7, 1950," December 25, 2005. http://NevadaObserver.com.

New Jersey Superior Court, Appellate Division. *Miller v. Bill Miller's Riviera Inc.* Decided August 6, 1952. http://nj.findacase.com.

New York Times. "Ben Marden, 77 Who Owned the Riviera Nightclub, Is Dead." N.d.

Paskevich, Michael. "Donn Arden: Master of Disaster." The First 100, part 3, A City in Full. *Las Vegas Review Journal*. www.1st100.com/part3/ arden.html.

Rose, Frank. *The Agency: William Morris and the Hidden History*. New York: HarperCollins, 1996.

Shapiro, Athur, Riviera physician. Personal interview with authors, May 18, 2011. Dr. Shapiro currently resides in Las Vegas, Nevada.

Sinatra, Nancy. *Frank Sinatra: An American Legend*. Mount Kisco, NY: Reader's Digest Association, 1998.

United States District Court District of New Jersey. *Bierman v. Marcus*. Opinion of the court was delivered by Modarelli, March 12, 1956.

Ward, James. *Architects in Practice New York City 1900–1940, for the Committee for the Preservation of Architectural Records, questionnaire for Architects Qualified for Federal Public Works*. Accessed through the American Institute of Architects files.

Werth, Barry. *Banquet at Delmonico's: Great Minds, the Gilded Age, and the Triumph of Evolution in America*. New York: Random House, 2009.

Yeshiva University. "Albert Einstein College of Medicine: A Brief History." New York: self-published, n.d.

INDEX

ABOUT THE AUTHORS

Tom Austin has spent his lifetime pursuing artistic endeavors. However, in his business life, he was recently awarded the coveted title of "Realtor Emeritus" by the National Association of Realtors in Washington, D.C., in recognition of more than forty years of outstanding contributions to the real estate industry. Tom has written dozens of published songs, the most popular being an international hit called "Short Shorts" that he cowrote with Bob Gaudio. He has recorded as an artist on ABC Paramount, Capitol and Old Town, as well as many other labels over the years. He is credited with writing the music for the Cleo Award–winning Nair commercial. Tom and his band, known as the "Royal Teens," have toured with everyone from Buddy Holley and the Crickets to Paul Anka, the Everly Brothers and Jerry Lee Lewis. The stage clothes Tom wore back in the 1950s are on permanent display at the Rock and Roll Hall of Fame in Cleveland, Ohio. Currently, "Short Shorts" is featured in the Tony Award–winning Broadway show *Jersey Boys*. Tom excels in painting in oils, watercolors and pen and ink drawings. Five of his nautical paintings are part of the permanent collection of the United States Coast Guard in Washington, D.C. Tom is currently the resident artist at the prestigious Salmagundi Club in New York. Contact Tom Austin at www.tomaustingallery.com and www.theroyalteens.com.

Ron Kase is an applied or public sociologist who has written books and articles, edited collections and consulted on a variety of social issues and social programs, as well as for policy creation venues. He is also a novelist, writing conspiracy stories resulting in three published novels (*Fiddler's Elbow*,

Fiddler's Revenge and *Fiddler's Return*), which have been optioned for motion picture development. He is writing a new novel set in Tampa, Florida's Ibor City in the 1930s, the former site of the Cuban cigar industry in America. Ron has been a sociology professor, senior college and university administrator, magazine publisher and local history writer. Currently, he directs the Sponsored Research Office (SRO) at a New Jersey state college. Contact Ron Kase at rjkase@gmail.com.